CW00455782

By Request

By Request

Isabella Mason Kirk

Illustrations by John Garth Wilkinson

Copyright © Isabella Mason Kirk 2012

First published in 2012 by Scotforth Books
on behalf of the author

www.scotforthbooks.com

All rights reserved
Unauthorised duplication contravenes existing laws

ISBN 978-1-904244-81-3

Designed and typeset by Carnegie Book Production

Printed and bound in the UK by Halstan Printing Group, Amersham

For my dear late husband Michael, my loving family – Michael, John, Isabel and Alice, who are always there for me, and all my good friends over the years.

Foreword

The Kirk family invited me to write an introduction to this collection of Bella's poems and I do so gladly.

We have been friends for nigh on four decades, which is a fair chunk of life. At the end of the 50s and through two thirds of the 60s, we were neighbours. In addition, for all my years in West Calder and Polbeth, I was privileged to be part of major family events.

Bella Kirk possesses manifold gifts – from ingeniously making and mending, to acting and composing verse. In her inimitable way she has entertained and encouraged a huge number of people in and around West Calder and beyond. She has produced poems for all seasons.

It was George Orwell who said that people cannot abide poetry because they associate it with what can't be understood. He went on to say that the word 'poetry' creates in advance the same sort of impression as the word God or a parson's dog-collar. He argues that poetry should be normalised via comprehensibility.

Bella Kirk normalises via comprehensibility. She writes with sense, sensibility and genuine sympathy for the human condition. Her verses ring bells because they have to do with people, places and experiences which are familiar. Thus as we absorb we are enriched. And as we absorb we appreciate that she writes as she does because she knows life, and she knows life in part because down the years she has enjoyed the company of others, and, equally significant, her own company. We recollect how she pushed her own children and her grandchildren along the quieter roads and not all that much used tracks bounding her community. As she walked she observed, using her observations to write material in her head before transferring it to paper.

No matter where she has recited publicly – in Harburn Hall or Polbeth Hall, in a Home for the not so young or a sheltered housing complex, in Harburn Golf Course Clubhouse or from the pulpit of Polbeth-Harwood Church – Bella has been welcomed and in a real sense has taught her hearers the truths obvious and not quite so obvious. In her verse, one finds the extraordinary in the ordinary.

When she occupied the pulpit in Polbeth during my annual vacation I was reminded of what the BBC's Religious Affairs Correspondent, Gerald Priestland, said in his autobiography. He quoted his successor, Rosemary Harthill, who remarked: *"I think I have learned more about God from the poems of George Herbert (who lived 400 years ago) than from all the sermons I have ever heard."*

This book will bring back memories to her family, her friends, her fans. How good that it has been produced. I am certain that with me you want to say to Bella words of thanks for her friendship and for the pleasure her poems have given and will give her friends.

D.K. Robertson, 1997

Reproduced from a previous publication with the kind permission of the family of the Late Reverend D. K. Robertson

Cauther in its Prime

To the tune of Dae ye mind on Lang Lang Syne?

Dae ye mind o' auld lang syne?
When Cauther was in its prime
Westwood Works and Addiewell
West Mains and Number Nine?
Dae ye mind the Poly Hall?
Where we gathered one and all
And danced the night through till the morning

Dae ye mind the Happy Land?
Where lived the greatest worthies in the land
Mossend, Gavieside and Shuttleha'?
Now only in our memory stand

Westwood House

Dae ye mind o' Harrit Row, Raeburn
Breich, Oakbank, them a'?
And walking ower the drove loan in the morning

Dae ye mind Pie Jock and his pies?
Nanny Mullens picture hoose? Oh, my
The chummy seats in the back row
It brings tears tae yer eyes
Noo they are nae mair, Cauther's no' the same, I'm shair
As ye walk doon the street in the morning

Dae ye mind the wee auld shops?
Nan Duncan's watches, rings and clocks
The Beehive and the Buttercup
Dick Mullen's wee fruit shop
McCowatt's high-class millinery
Mick Murray's wee shop tae?
Where ye got yer Woodbines
And yer papers every morning

Dae ye mind o' J D Brown the printer
The Blacksmith shop, the auld smiddy
Lipton's and Kearsley the cobbler
At the top o' the Cleugh Brae?
Santini and Tapaldi, they came here frae Italy
Noo instead o' sunshine they get rain every morning

Dae ye mind o' Gillon's licensed corner shop
The personal service that ye got?
And Grant's vanilla slices, they just could'na be forgot
The big Co-op gala day, the weans shouting hip-hooray
As they marched doon the street in the morning

Dae ye mind auld Johnny Boyle's billiard ha'?
A meeting place for a'

The chaff was great and the atmosphere
As the players hit the ba'
Noo you watch it on the screen
It goes on for weeks, it seems
Until the wee sma' hours o' the morning

Dae ye mind the auld high school
Where ye were taught by rod and rule?
Cauther Street on divi-day
Annie Wilson's wee tea-shop packed full
Aye, ye don't half miss the Co-op
When you need a new claes rope
Or a teapot for yer tea in the morning

Dae ye mind auld Tommy's barber shop
The razors then, yon big cut-throat?
And Sneddon's, if you once got in
Was an Aladdin's cave, I aye thought
Watson's ironmongery was right across the way
A' daen brisk business in the morning

Dae ye mind o' Cauther Sports
The procession and the floats?
The streets were lined wi' folk and weans
Some o' them gie wee tots
Jack Sleigh and his china stand
Hobby horses and pipe bands
And the sair heids ye had in the morning

Dae ye mind Tam Halliday the butcher?
A right auld wag was he
And Wilson's fish shop in Union Street
Where you got kippers for your tea
McBryns bicycle shop, where ma Raleigh bike I bought
That was a long time ago in the morning

POLY HALL & THISTLE TOWER, West Cowther

Dae ye mind the auld polis station?
Next door was Ogilvey
And whit's his name, ye mind Auld Wheesht
Frae the local library
Kate Tennant's quaint auld shop
Where as a lassie I aye got
Ma pencils for the school in the morning

Dae ye mind the nine-penny rattler
The good auld puffy train?
Packed wi' local lads and lassies
Frae the big toon coming hame
Well, the station it's still there
Now it's one pound forty single fare
Tae get ye back hame tae Cauther in the morning

Dae ye mind the auld lodging hoose?
The model was another name
A place o' rest for travelling folk

And casual workers far frae hame
A bed for the tattie howkers
Dry-stane dykers till they moved
On their way doon the street in the morning

A', weel, I suppose things hae aye tae change
But it's nice tae bring tae mind
The way things were when we were young
And we were in oor prime
We aye mind the good auld days
And a' the freens we made
And the ones we'll meet again in the morning

Touring Scotland
with Wullie, Myra, Hans & Patsy

The first day of our holidays, we spent at Lochearnhead
Where we watched the water ski-ing after everyone was fed
Later on we pitched our tent, near Loch Tula for the night
When the farmer came an' told us, there's a wild bull out of sight

We've seen auld Scotland's hills and glens
Her castles and her buts an' bens
We waited hours to cross the Stromeferry
And in that time the men got merry

At last we crossed to the other side
And camped upon a lone hillside
That night it rained and the wind it blew
We thought our holiday was through

We packed our bags to leave the west
To travel east might prove the best
For we'd been told by passers-by
That in the east was a clear blue sky
A herd of deer we saw that day
A wonderful sight for the bairns to see

We travelled on and camped once more
Near Invergordon, by a breezy shore
The weather there was simply grand
We'd a dip in the sea and a game on the sand

Next day, we went to visit Dingwall
While Myra and Wullie watched camp for us all
We saw a porpoise out in the sea
Swimming away right merrily

Here we spent another night and it went without a hitch
But in the morning as we left, we landed in the ditch
Still further on along our way
A puncture Hans did have that day

As Wullie went to lend a hand
He found his pants would not expand
The wheel was changed, his trousers sewn
We had a good laugh and then got going

The road to Ullapool was a glorious sight
And in the nearby camping ground we spent the night
We motored on and stopped again for tea by the side of the road
Where young Ian fell and near killed himself while playing
    in the wood

All of us got quite a fright for the time being
But taking all in afterwards, Hans was worse than Ian
Then on again near Aviemore we bedded down our flock
But oh, dear me, the midges there bit us quite a lot

We finished up our holiday
By visiting Pitlochry
By that time Hans had gone on home
So our lunchtime there we had alone
We went a walk right through the dam
In which the lovely salmon swam

We are now on our journey home
We've seen a lot of sights
The bairns have had a few mishaps
The men some jolly nights
We've all enjoyed the open air, the sunshine and the rain
But if we're spared another year we'll do the same again

1958

The Farmers Nowadays

I would like to try and tell ye how farming ways have changed
For by joves, things are different noo frae what they were
   in olden days
A farmer's work nowadays isna' what it was
An' I'll just try and tell you the reason why because

Instead o' milking coos by hand it's a' done by machines
An' instead of sacky aprons, they're a' dressed up in jeans
They've got combines for their harvesting an' spreaders
   for their dung
An' work that used to take twa weeks is noo a' done in one

The hens are in wee cages, they ca' them batteries
The coos are served by test tube means, nae need for nature's ways
An' even in the kitchen there are machines for washing dishes
Washing claes and mixing cakes or anything one wishes

The farmer an' his wife gaein jaunting in their cars
Dining oot at posh hotels, jist like film stars
They're at whist drives, young farmers' clubs, in fact they're never in
An' they'll try and tell ye their work is never duin

There are subsidies for this an' that, and grants for buts and bens
An' like as no' a few things mair, the likes o' us don't ken
They're maybe early risers an' they're oot in rain and shine
But maist of farmers nowadays never had a better time

November 1963

Harburn Clubhouse

Noo, if you'll a' just gather roon, I'll tell ye a' a tale
It concerns a certain clubhouse, by the name o' Hardale
It's had its share o' bad luck, as perhaps ye may recall
A fire destroyed the premises, a black day for us all

Since the willing hands o' men too numerous tae name
Have finished the gigantic task of re-building it again
And to the ladies a word of praise is longsyne overdue
For their generous donation and hard work the whole year through

There are many people here tonight who don't play golf at a'
And they wouldn't ken the difference 'tween a tattie and a ba'
But at the socials you'll be sure tae find them gathered here
It must be for the company, or maybe it's the beer

I hear three times, members here, have had a hole in one
So gents, take note and try to find exactly hoo it's done
You'll get presented with a putter and bottle o' the best
And from then on you'll always be a very welcome guest

And the talent that you find up here I'm sure you'll a' agree
Is better than some programmes they've dished up on TV
Then there's always the one-armed bandit, if you've any cash to spare
You never know your luck, folks, the jackpot might be there

You've got young folk an' auld folk here, their age I darena' mention
They're even playing golf up here, and due the auld age pension
And the game is very popular with the ladies now it seems
They add a bit of glamour, when putting on the greens

As far as I can understand, there's eighteen holes to play
But the fifteenth hole, it's nameless and the worst, or so they say
Others include the Beeches, the Faulds and Cobbinshaw
Just a few I've mentioned, I couldna name them a'

So all you men tak heed noo, ye better watch your score
For from noo on it's going to be the ladies who are shouting FORE
Though ma man he's no golfer, my son has joined the ranks
And for many social evenings here, may we say, many thanks

1963

Jenny Russell

Now there's nae need to tell you folks, hairdressing is my trade
George is in the Insurances, that's how our fortune's made
And also as a sideline, I'm an agent for foundations
I measure up the female form to their specifications

I get folk with far too many curves and some with nane at a'
They've got bulges in places I wish I never saw
They get fitted out with uplifts and belts you cannae
When on, tell the difference frae teenagers to their grannies

Then you get them in for Beatle cuts, razor cuts and a'
They go out of here with hairstyles that would drive you up the wa'
But I'm coining in the money and it's no' for me to say
As long as they are satisfied, well, let them stay that way

And of course I couldn'na close my verse without a word as well
About a certain friend of mine, as well kent as myself

He's an elder in the Kirk out here, you'd think he owned the place
The way he bosses us about, it is a right disgrace

Even at the Agapay, or anything at all
He's always saying, Mind noo, look after my wee hall
I would'na put it past him, he acts the part that well
To say the minister is indisposed and take the stand himsel'

I've not found out just what he does, he works somewhere at Thynes
He could be on the directors' board, with wages double mine
Whatever he does, he's gie hard worked, we ken without a doubt
But Andy's willing services we couldna dae without

1963

Bellsquarry

Bellsquarry at one time was mainly buts and bens
A typical country village, where folk kept a wheen o' hens
It has its ain wee village school and pub that's fine and near
And then there's aye the cattle show, it's held here once a year

There's a wee shop-come-post-office, it's used by one and all
And of course we just couldn't forget Bellsquarry's ain wee hall
For it's there they hold their functions, socials and the like
And you're always made that welcome, just as we are tonight

There's no' much entertainment, but it's lovely countryside
And if it's peace and quiet you're after, it's the ideal place tae bide
But the wind o' change is blowing and it won't be long, they say
Till the new town of Livingston is coming up this way

There'll be new houses, schools and factories, springing up
  where there is space
Bringing some employment, that is much needed round the place
It will likely bring in other things, but I hope one thing remains
That's the contentment that you find here, may it always be the same

1964

Ian & Trudi Prentice's Housewarming

Now, Ian and Trudi, for the first two to three years of their marriage
Lived in a wee hoose right next to the garage
It was really quite old and the outlook gie tumbledoon
So they flitted up to a more select part o' the toon

Up beside all the gentry next to the hoose Ower-the-wa'
And we're here tonight to sort of welcome them a'
Long may their lum reek and God bless their new home
I just wonder, though, if they realise what they've taen on

For as this was once a manse, they'll have to be awfully good
You know, always remember to say grace before eating their food
Oh, they'll have to show a good example and lead a good life
Ian, always turn the other cheek when fighting with the wife

And remember the Commandments, treat thy neighbour well
Bring ower your mower and cut their grass, or you'll all go tae hell
And when Jock's pheasants come ower and leave their trademarks
  on the windowsill
Keep in your mind the fifth commandment, remember thou shalt
  not kill

Do no sinful action, and do not curse or swear
Even though you've tripped and fell half-roads down that stair
Be fruitful and multiply like the good book tells you to
And watch and dinna spread the germ, it's a wee bit like the flu
And six days shalt thou make love, every day including Monday
But always remember, never, never on a Sunday

1964

Kirk Brothers

Michael and Wullie, or better known as the Kirk Brothers
Are the friendliest of partners, in business and all other
Pastimes they indulge in, from choir practice up to darts
I'm sure you'll all agree with me, they are a perfect match

I know it's nice they are like that, and never show the rag
In fact it's the other way round, it's the wives that are inclined to nag
And when they've got a man to see, it always takes the two
And very often you will find, they come home late and fu'

They've always got excuses, no matter what we say
They really meant to be home, but they could'na get away
At times they take us with them, they're really no' that bad
And they work gie hard, we ken that, but at times they make us mad

Like the time they went to the base, with McDonald's social club
They were home again by twelve o'clock, but at four still in the pub
Or the time they went to estimate the damage at the Vaults
Tam Gillespie brought them home, but of course it could'na be
    their fault

Kirk Brothers

They were only testing whisky to see if it was damaged by the fire
And of course it had taen them baith, these twa you must admire
They share their pleasures, problems too, and whatever comes
    their way
But I know they'll do the same again, whatever we may say

We're no' complaining really, we're gie well off, that's true
And if at times we're awkward, we don't blame it all on you
There's just one thing I'd like to say and get it off my mind
Michael, dear, and Wullie, dear, will you no' come home on time?

February 1964

Crombie's Milk Laddie (Oor John)

Since the Summer I hae taen a job, I'm Crombie's wee milk laddie
And if you listen carefully, you're bound to hear my barrae
I rise up at half past six and get started on my round
While maist the folk are still in bed and likely sleeping sound

But I aye meet up with somebody and I gie them all a nod
And if they're going my way, I chum them up the road
Och aye, there's always something that's sure to interest me
A wee brown rabbit or a blackie in a tree

It's also beneficial to my pocket and my health
I've bought myself a single bed with all my hard-earned wealth
You see, I get a better sleep and I'm fresher when I rise
So there's something in yon saying, To be healthy, wealthy and wise

Then I bought a fishing rod I've had my eye on for a while
And I think of all the fish I'll catch as I trudge along each mile
Before I ken just where I am I'm finished for the day
Another morning nearer Saturday, that's when I get my pay

November 1964

Oor John in London with Rev. D. K. Robertson

Mind a telt you last year, about my wee bit job?
I'm going to tell you where it taen me, plus all they extra bobs
It was the Minister's idea really, John, he says to me
If you can get yoursel' tae London, we'll gie you lodgings free
I ken he's a man who means every word he says
And well! Ye ken yourself what lodgings are these days

I'm no' a chap that would let a chance like that go by
And seeing I was tae get my lodgings free, I might just afford to fly

But, alas, they wanted far ower much, sixteen pounds to be exact
And my money was o'er hard-earned to blow it all like that
So I went on the Flying Scotsman, for little mair than thirty bob
And I had lunch going through Darlington, I was treated like a lord
Mind you, it cost fourteen and sixpence, I had a three course lunch
    the lot
The waiter always called me sir, that's what money does, I thought
I soon reached Kings Cross Station and I was pleased to see
Mr Robertson and family, all waiting there for me

They took me all round London, to places I had heard about
I saw Big Ben and London Bridge and we aye had coffee out
We went lots of picnics in the parks, with Susie and wee Jane
And went shopping in Harrods, if you please, for presents
    to take hame
The week soon passed and the time came round for my holiday
    to end
There was nae lunch on the journey back, all my money I had spent
My good freens gave me sandwiches, they're folk I'll aye admire
I'll hae tae gie a generous donation when the Minister retires

1964

Ode tae Andra

You'll have heard about Andra Graham, you all know who I mean
It's well known that his work's all done by his weans
    and a' their freens

He encourages them to bring them doon especially at weekends
And the puir wee souls are set to work feeding calves
　　and mucking pens

I'm talking from experience, oor John will bear me oot
For he worked down at Gavieside six years or there aboot
He was jist a wee bit skinny lad when he first went doon there
He had led a very sheltered life and had never learnt to swear
He was telt tae gie the coos their turnips and telt, Noo, dinna tarry!
And the puir wee soul tho' he did his best, he couldnae shove
　　the barrae!

And the fly auld Andra, dae ye ken whit he telt the loon?
That if he supped his porridge every day, before the new moon
He would shove the turnip barrae, so he never missed a day
He found he could shove the barrae nae bother, hip, hip, hooray!

It turned out Andra had oiled the barrae, unknown to the lad
Although John never kent that, Andra fairly had him had
And as the lads got older, he'd gie them different jobs
It helped to boost their egos, plus an occasional two or three bob

Then they'd get a promotion to drive the tractor, considered quite
　　a treat
But the greatest honour bestowed on them, was to get a shot
　　at Andra's Jeep
I couldn't count the lads that Andra knocked into shape
He would kick their arse or cuff their ear, but the weans all
　　thought him great

In fact, I've come to this conclusion, and I believe without a doot
That in John's years doon at Gavieside, he learnt mair than
　　from a book!

Stornoway

To the tune of the same name

We've been up to Stornoway
And we've been to Oronsay
That's where we spent our holiday
In lovely Stornoway

It's an isle of many lochs and bays
With fish in every loch, they say
It also rains there every day
In lovely Stornoway

There's wee peat stacks along the way
And quaint wee hooses thatched wi' hay
On Sunday all they do is pray
In lovely Stornoway

They take life up there come what may
They don't mind if the skies are grey
Tomorrow there's another day
In lovely Stornoway

No matter where our footsteps strayed
Many teuchter freens we made
Come back again, they always said
To lovely Stornoway

So we'll go back another day
And spend another holiday
Among the peaceful scenery
Of lovely Stornoway

1964

Rabbie Burns – Harburn Golf Club

Every year about this time, the thoughts of Scotsmen turn
And they meet to toast the memory of the immortal Rabbie Burns
They partake of what we all ken was a typical Scottish dish
A heaped plate of haggis, which is neither fowl nor fish
Of course, with champit tatties and neeps all nice and warm
And with a feed like that inside you, you'll no' come to any harm

There's also cheese and bannocks, and once you're satisfied
They drink a toast and tell how long it is since Rabbie died
They also toast the lassies of whom our lad was fond
T'was to them he wrote his songs of love, as by the banks of Ayr
    he roamed
A lot's been said of Rabbie, he was handsome, young and gay
And there's nae doubt he was gifted in many different ways

His poems and songs, still famous yet, even after all these years
Songs that reach your very heart and fill your een wi' tears
He had his share of happiness and also sorrow too

And they say he drank with all his cronies, gie aft
    the whole night through
But though he was born of humble folks, as often great men are
His fame still shines as brightly yet, as in the song, his star

Noo, I wonder if our Rab had been here in the present day
Do ye think he would have been inclined a game of golf to play?
I can see him on the fairway noo, his golf club in his hand
While a' the time he's wondering where his ball is going to land

Will it land fair and square in the middle o' the green
Or away amongst the rough, where it's no' easy to be seen?
In that case, he'd be quite a while looking for the thing
He'd nae time to compose a verse or two, perhaps Jim Spiers
    could sing

But I don't think that he'd hae had the time this relaxing game to play
He seems to have used leisure hours in an entirely different way
There's one thing, though, the lassies here would have
    inspired him just the same
And he might have lived a wee bit longer, had he played the
    golfing game

The Moose

These last twa, three days I've had a guest in oor hoose
You'll hae had yin yirsel', it's a cheeky wee moose
I first made its acquaintance when I went for a knife
It jumped oot o' the drawer, I got the fright of ma life
The next time it appeared ahint the bread bin
Then disappeared in among where I keep the spuins
Says I tae masel' I'd best get a trap
For I had a sneaking suspicion it was looking gie fat

I sent one of the weans a trap for tae buy
And I taen everything oot but nae moose did I spy
So I scrubbed oot the place and feeling gie pleased
I pit doon the trap wi' a bit of red cheese
I then washed the doorstep for it was guid soapy water
And when I put the pail back I let it doon wi' a clatter
For believe it or no' the cheese was away
But I'll catch that moose yet, if it's the last thing I dae

I hauled oot the fridge in case it was there
There was a bicycle pump and of all things I declare
A half pun o' marg that had fell doon the back

But nae sign of the moose, it was quick off the mark
So I re-set the trap, the same thing happened again
I'll say this for the moose, by joves it was game
As a matter of fact, I've no' got it yit
If the worst comes tae the worst, I'll just need to flit

But the next night I went oot and when I got back
The poor wee cratur was caught in the trap
I felt awfy sad it had to dee in ma hoose
For after a', life is precious to even a moose

March 1965

Holiday in Majorca

You'll hae heard about Majorca, it's an island just off Spain
Wi' Jean and Andra, we all set off a month ago away frae all the rain
To spend a week just lazing and soaking up the sun
And wine and dine in the best hotel and generally hae a week of fun

So we set off one Sunday afternoon to catch a plane at Abbotsinch
And when aboard our B.E.A. we got settled doon at once
With our rations o' cheap cigs and, of course, brandy tae
In no time we were at Palma airport three hundred miles away

What a difference in the weather when we stepped off that plane
We could hardly believe three hours ago we had set off in the rain
In no time we were installed in this lovely new hotel
So we all got settled in and vowed we would enjoy oursel'

That very night we chanced to meet two auld freens frae hame
Who promptly took us out to Lits bar to sample the champagne
Boy, did we have fun that night, that was the night of nights
Michael ended up hanging on to a lamp-post lit up underneath
    its light

We got him and his bosom pal bunged into a taxi cab
And although Andra could'na mind a thing, he was sure that
    he'd been had
In the lift we shoved them before they could change their minds
And folks, I'm no' telling you a lie, we went up and doon in it
    seven times

Every time it stopped we'd try and slide the door, but all in vain
Then Andra would press the button and away we'd go again
I really thought cooped up inside, for the night we'd hae to stay
When Michael staggered up against the door, and it opened
    out the way

23

Next day Andra could'na mind a thing, his face was awful pale
While Michael on the other hand, looked as if he'd been in
   a force ten gale
We took it easy that day and at night before we dined
We thought we'd all hae a shower to help us tae unwind

So we agreed to meet a' the gether up in oor hotel room
And hae a duty free hauf before we all went doon
The first to arrive up was Andra in dire need of a hauf
Just wait till I tell you what happened, he'd slipped going in the bath
He says that he stood on a wee bit o' soap, too wee it could'na be seen
But my personal opinion is, he slipped while chasing Jean

Anyway folks, I can tell you for days he was black and blue
He says that the last time he was as bad as that, he had been
   kicked by an Ayrshire coo
And he never again felt inclined to go and take a shower
He just got his face cloth and had a dicht all ower

And being Andra he took the episode all in his stride
There wasna much visible bruising, it being mostly all on his backside
But I must admit I laughed until my sides were sair
And everytime I looked ower at Andra, I laughed a' the mair

Then one day we decided we would hire a wee car for the day
We could go to Porto Cristo and see the caves on the way
I was all for a wee car with the roof that rolled back
But Andra thought we'd be safer with a solid roof
In case we happened to stoat off the track

And folks, you might not believe this what I'm going to say
But somehow or other we managed to get onto a runway

Seemingly it was a new runway – unfinished as of yet
An extension to Palma airport, intended for the Jumbo Jet

It was meant to be opened early in the New Year
Says Andra, we'd better get to hell out of here
How we managed to get on it, I never will know
It's a good job there was nae aircraft flying in low

We had a good tour of Majorca that day
We enjoyed every minute, that I will say
So we tried to get back before darkness fell
For we'd to pass Palma airport again to get back to our hotel

We did'na get back the way we had planned
Like the planes, we circled the airport twice, I thought we were
    coming in to land
It was Andra's first time driving on the wrong side of the road
But he got us all safely back to Campa Stella, thank God

Then another ploy we got up to, it was definitely a laugh
We went sightseeing on donkeys away up some mountain path
We were with another company, about thirty folk in all
We set off up this mountain path with my wee donkey, last of a'

It really was awful funny, it let every other donkey past
It certainly was no Nijinsky for the blooming thing was last
I could stand here all night though, telling you about our holiday
But I think I'd better finish an' let someone else hae their say

In the meantime I'm trying to reform Michael to stop smoking
    and spend his Saturday nights at hame
And the money that he does'na spend, we'll hae another week
    in Spain

Tammy Woods – First Annual Dance

There's nae need to tell you folks how Tammy's fortune's made
For he must be near a millionaire since he started in the motor trade
Well, first of all, he started way back in nineteen-fifty-six
By re-roofing an old smiddy, altering it a bit

Things were doing away all right, but he thought he might go far
So he took the plunge in fifty-nine and started selling motor cars
Nae less than fifteen cars passed through his hands that year
He also started Wullie Bryce, he's still head salesman here

Another of his right hand men from the central garage came
That was in nineteen-sixty and Jim Drummond was his name
Since then he has acquired a staff that is fairly large
That means now Mrs Woods can bake with butter instead of marg

This year he extended and taen ower Paton's shop
But let me say the farmers here boost his trade a lot
Them with a' their money, they change their cars each year
It's no' everyone can manage that, certainly no' the tradesmen here

But dare I say, it has never been plain sailing all the way
That's made the East End Garage what it is the day
But let me say it's awfu' nice to see Tammy make the grade
And I hope he'll always prosper in the good old motor trade

1965

Thomasina

It was a cauld wintry night it appeared at oor place
A wee stray kitten hungry and thin
It looked that pathetic and had such a taking wee face
The weans said, Oh, gonnae let it in

At first I just said gie it something to eat
But I'm definitely no' keeping a cat
You ken fine we've got enough for to keep
And I've made up my mind, noo that's that

There was a good going chorus frae the weans of, Oh, Maw!
The pair wee thing's chilled through and through
And forby, it's too wee to bide oot in the snow
Gaun, let it into the fire just the noo

So needless to say, it got itsel' wangled in
And was treated like some V.I.P
The dog wisnae pleased, it gave some gie dirty looks
At the kitten curled up on their knee

It wisnae what you'd say an awful braw cat
It was sort of a dark tortoiseshell
With a wee white waistcoat and paws, and in fact
I found I quite liked it mysel'

So I said it could bide till we found it a hame
The weans said, Oh, Maw, you're a pal
Do you think Thomasina would be a good name?
And we'll find it a hame, so we will

They patted and pampered that wee pussy cat
It kept them amused, that's for sure
But they never found it a hame, and in fact
The wee pussy cat is still here

Thomasina's grown up noo
And turned a right bonnie cat
And had offers of marriage, an' a'
Frae very respectable tom cats as well
But we advised her to turn doon them all

So she had a wee operation, it cost thirty-five shillings
Plus the bus fares to the vet at East Cauther
He said to call back at seven, I'll have finished the job
And with suitors you'll have nae further bother

So we got the wee cat back, its stitches oot a week later
It didnae budge fae the fire all the same
But noo it's in with the bricks and an amusing wee creature
Aye, Thomasina at last found a hame

1965

Ho-Ro-Ho-Rea

To the tune of the same name

Ho-ro-ho-rea, we've been to Tiree
An isle of green grass and sea breezes
Where you walk for miles and view the Isles
Of buttercups and daisies

Tam's hoose was braw, there was room for us a'
We'd every home comfort, really
The folk there were kind, had oor welfare in mind
Especially Wullie and Mary

When we arrived at the pier, Wullie said, You've got here
Had you a good trip over?
I'm Wullie McPhee from the Isle of Tiree
I'm afraid I've had more than one over

There's Joe Neil and me and Johnny makes three
We're like the birds of a feather
Through sunshine and rain, you'll find us the same
Many a storm we have weathered

But joking apart, the isle gets your heart
And though I've travelled all over
There's one place for me, it's the Isle of Tiree
When my wandering days are all over

I'll buy me a hoose and a wee boat forby
And sail when the wind's in my favour
In its sheltering bays, spend the rest of my days
On the Isle of Tiree and its neighbours

The Glebe Singers

Here is a tale best telt by mysel'
For who else knows the Glebe Singers that well?
They're a group of male singers, whose one aim in life
Is to spend as much time as they can away from the wife

It's their custom to practice at least once a week
For a couple of hours, then they're off down the street
McDonald's, I think, is their favourite place
And it's aye near eleven before they show face

There's ten in the group, with various trades
It would take too long to tell how their fortunes are made
But I gie credit where credit is due
This double male quartet has won honours too

Their singing's a pleasure, without doubt we enjoy
Their now-famous rendering of The Farmer's Boy
There's nothing they like better than a drop of the craitur
With a good going sing-song to follow on later

Oh, they've aye got excuses for nights out together
And it's amazing the storms they all manage to weather
But joking apart, I must say something nice
They'd make an interesting subject for This Is Your Life

Going for Sticks

Now, folks, I've got a pastime I'd like to tell you a' aboot
It doesn't cost a penny and, you see, it takes me oot
It's gathering sticks up in the wood, it's relaxing, I would say
And the time of year I like the best is April or the month of May

For after hibernating for the winter, while others take up golf
    and bools
I just get ma wee go-cart oot and when the weans are at the school
I get masel' way up the road and, of course, I take my wee dug tae
It likes a romp up in Walkers' Woods, it would bide up there a' day

I often come upon a wee bird's nest, I ken the places for tae look
All snug and cosy lined with earth and wool, a work of art
    without a doot
And whilst I see a rabbit with his wee white fluffy tail
And I also always pass the post van going to Tarbrax with the mail

Then I see the wee violets growing in amangst the grass
I look for this every year, they're awfae bonnie while they last
And, of course, trees are always interesting, like folk, never two
    the same
Although every year they grow older, they never seem to change

Oh, aye, I like to go for sticks, that's a hobby I've acquired
So I hope I'm spared a long time yet to go and gather sticks
Apart frae enjoying the beauty o' the countryside, it helps tae keep
  me fit

The Hoose Ower The Wa'

By starting this story first let me explain
How we came to build a wee hoose o' oor ain
Oor auld hoose was too wee, there wasnae room for us a'
So we thought we would build yin jist ower the wa'

There was a grand skelp of grund, wi' eight muckle trees
Where the laddies had torn all their breeks and their knees
And Michael, he said, If they trees were awa'
There's room for a hoose there, jist ower the wa'

So we applied to the Kirk for tae purchase the land
It was duly consented, things were working out grand
We taen doon the trees, it was hard work wi' a saw
Aye, and we taen doon the telegraph wires an' a'

Then Michael got busy and drew oot a plan
And informed all oor freens we wid need a bit hand
Then Ross Contractor came in and levelled it a'
But first we'd to knock a hole in the wa'

Then we got the founds dug and the bricks ready to lay
Sammy Holmes built them up and his mate helped him tae
They soon slapped them up, twas nae bother at a'
And before you could wink there was a hoose ower the wa'

It was the joiners turn noo to show us their skill
But they werna long started when Michael taen ill
Appendix, they said, and they whipped him awa'
In the middle of flooring the hoose ower the wa'

Young Michael and Sammy started where he left aff
And had the hoose floored while you could cough
Then they struck a problem, it near stumped them a'
They couldnae find a sewer for the hoose ower the wa'

They dug up that road three times, I'm shair
They would have been doon to Australia if they'd dug ony mair
In fact, I thought they would never find it at a'
That we'd need a wee hoose for that hoose ower the wa'

The hoose was noo finished an' ready to paint
We thought it looked well, it was money well spent
So we all got stuck in, Myra and Wullie an' a'
We had to keep the cost doon in the hoose ower the wa'

The great day arrived for us to move digs
Me and Michael, four weans and wee Midge
A goldfish, a cat, four bantams an' a'
To take up abode in the hoose ower the wa'

It taen us two years to build but we're in it at last
We've plenty of room and hot water to wash
And when we're asked whit we cried it, I might as well tell you a'
We couldnae think of anything else but The Hoose Ower The Wa

1965

Guising – Mikey, John, Issy & Ali in Aid of Aberfan Disaster

To the tune of 'My old man's a dustman'

I'd like to be a wee nurse in Emergency Ward Ten
I'd take oot your appendix and send you hame again
Or I'll maybe help the dentist giving gas and air
And watch you while you're sitting shaking in the dentist's chair

I'd like to be a joiner when I leave the school
I'll build wee huts and garages and I'll always work to rule
I'll also help the doctor out, I'll be sure to please
I'll fix you up with wooden legs with hinges at the knees

I think I'll chance my luck and go upon the stage
But I don't think I've got the figure, nor come to that, the face
I'll have to earn my living somehow, a hairdresser I could be
And fix you up with hairstyles, to believe, you'd really need to see

Oh, I think I'll be a policeman like Dixon of Dock Green
I'd put away the naughty boys where they could never more be seen
Or I'll maybe be a banker and treat the money like my ain
And every year I can afford to holiday in Spain

I'd like to be a teacher when I grow up one day
For it's the only blooming job I ken with eight weeks holiday
Or I'll maybe be a chorus girl and gie you all a treat
On second thought, I'd better no, I think I've two left feet

I think I'll be an air hostess and work for B.E.A.
You could be the pilot, we'd be fleeing night and day
Or I'll maybe be a pop star just like Sandie Shaw
Singing songs that send you, but it would be up the wa'

I'll maybe be a painter and paint my mammy's hoose
I'll also paint my granny's too, for the paper's hanging loose
I'll maybe be a postman, now that's the job for me
I'll read all the dirty postcards while I have my cup o' tea

I'd like to be a bus driver on a corporation bus
You could be my clippie, noo, that's the job for us
Or I'll maybe be a farmer with a herd of milking coos
On second thoughts I'd better no', I'd get sh**! a' o'er ma shoes

But whatever kind of job we choose, and whether it's done well
Life is what you make it, it's all up to oorsel'

1966

Alec Meikle's Barn Dance in Harburn Hall

Dae ye mind yon night? It was jist a year the noo
There was a big storm and the wind it blew
Weel it so happened a great big tree
Fell with a thud on the place where you pee

It was a terrible tragedy, in fact a real how-d'you-do
It created quite a problem and put the Harburn ladies in a stew
What they were going to dae without it, they really didnae ken
For ye a' agree on one point, women are jist no' built like men

When a man wants to spend a penny, it's jist like gaen to blow
    his nose
But a woman is slightly different, there's mair o' them exposed
Ye just canna ask a lady if she'd like to see a man about a dug
Ye'd end up wi'a jeely nose and she'd likely belt yer lug

So Alec Meikle couldn't haud his barn dance, it jist had to be delayed
And as funds were at their very lowest the work would have to
    be unpaid
And who was going to fix it? That was the big question o' the day
And it's well kent Alec was only skilled in building bales o' hay

But for Michael the hall held memories, for that's where he met
    with Bell
So he said for auld times sake, he'd build the place himsel'
Two, three Sundays he went an' gied up his precious time
And while he worked his thoughts went back to when
    he was in his prime

He enjoyed every minute, I'm sure it made him feel quite young
Thinking if only he could turn the clock back, my widna that be fun

So he got the hoose finished and wi' the help o' Wullie Brash
They completed a wee hoose, that you'll agree is jist first class
In fact I'd say without a doubt it's looking good as new
And the wee hoose had a great first night, judging by the queue

Noo, I'd like to add a postscript for a' you people here
Wullie Brash and Michael each received a bottle for their New Year
Their work didn'a go unnoticed and I'd like it understood
The bottle was from the ladies of the Rural with their thanks
    and gratitude

For although the hall is getting auld and a bit the worse for wear
They too wouldn't like to see it go doon, there've been some grand
    nights held up here
It's exactly a year last night frae that big tree did fall
But ye'll agree it will take mair than that tae finish Harburn Hall

1966

The Brashs' Hoose

You've heard aboot the Kirks' new hoose, the one cried
    Ower The Wa'
But hae ye heard aboot the Brashs? For they built ane an a'
They used to bide in Harburn Road but they were overcrowded tae
So they took the plunge and built a braw new hoose, only it was
    up the brae

I don't know who first thought of it, I expect it was much the same
    as us
With the family growing rapidly, a bigger hoose just was a must

And Chris just said tae Wullie, If the Kirks can we can tae
And ye ken I fancy staying up by Dr Walker's hoose just up the top
   of the brae

So Wullie saw Rab Russell and got things a' fixed up
And with visions o' a bigger hoose, Chris bought the weans a pup
They had nae wa' tae knock doon and nae beech trees in the way
You could say it was an ideal site for a hoose jist up the brae

Brogan Watson did the brickwork, the joiner work Watmore
Jimmy Morris did the plasterwork, while Chrissie scrubbed the floor
And of course Wullie did the plumbing work and Allan helped him tae
Along with a hundred other jobs in the hoose just up the brae

It didnae take them all that long, about a year I heard them say
But of course Wullie's golfing suffered, he just had nae time tae play
But I'm sure it was a labour of love frae it started tae it stopped
And I hope they'll a' be happy, in the hoose they cried Brae Top

Life begins at Forty

You'll a' hae heard the saying at forty life begins
Well, I wondered if it was true before, but noo I ken, by jings
For I hae joined the Women's Guild and the rural, I'm in that
And although I'm no' quite forty, at least I've made a start

For years I never crossed the door or ventured oot at a'
But noo the bairns are getting up and no' dependent on their maw
And faither's got his interests, the Glebe Singers and the darts
So I just thought it's time that I was getting off ma mark

Between a social evening noo and then, and a dance frae time to time
I never thought I'd stand the pace, but by joves I'm daen fine
I might even take up golfing yet, it relaxes you, I've heard
And it would always help to keep at bay what's known as
    middle-aged spread

For you've got to have a hobby or an interest of some kind
They say it helps to keep you healthy in body and in mind
They also say that life is sweet, enjoy it while you can
So noo I leave the dishes in the sink and dinna gie a dam

1966

On Holiday wi' Andra & Jean Graham

We arrived at Palma airport, last November at half past eight
Who was waiting there to greet us? Olaf at the gate
We nearly had heart failure, as a voice through the intercom
Boomed out, The Kirks are wanted, would you kindly come along?

So that night we had a party in whose room it wasn't hard to guess
But next morning I can tell you, Jean had to help me clean the mess
We nearly had tae get a tractor and trailer to take the empties all away
Empty bottles of J.B Rare, one of vodka and brandy tae
Eleven empty glasses, plus four empty bottles that held water
    brought frae hame
Ten mad Scots and one Dutchman had played the drinking game

It lasted till half past two in the morning, when we all called it a day
Michael and Andra got Olaf a taxi, saying, Thank God he's away
But next morning he appeared again as boisterous as could be
Andra even had to change his claes, Olaf pulled him in the sea

And at one point in the proceedings, beside the pool he picked up Jean
He was going to dump her in the deep end, if I had'na intervened

He took the Hotel El Cid by storm, by appearing in a kilt
A senorita with a beard, who sang Dark Island with a lilt
That day we'll all remember, it's fixed forever in our minds
But it took another night and day before we could unwind

The next night it was Ellen and Wullie's anniversary, they held it
    in their room
But Michael and I were absent, oor heids still had'na stopped
    going roon
But we heard the celebrations and laughs coming from through
    the wa'
As in true Scots tradition, they drank to their health and bairnies a'

I bet Wullie didn'a need his stick that night, he could have done
    the Highland Fling
A bit like Andy Pandy, a puppet on a string
Then we had a day donkey riding, we thought it would be a laugh
Fiona's one stood on her toes and Michael's tossed him aff

He skint his elbow, banged his heid, cried it every name
    under the sun
And vowed what he would dae to it if he only had a gun
And Andra's poor wee donkey looked that lean and just a bag o' bones
It was a bit like Delaney's donkey, it only wanted left alone
I think it was the one I had last year, the one that came in last
Only this time it had Andra on it, and it was me who got the laugh

And I must tell you about Marion, she taen a fancy for gateau
Every time she saw them in a shop, she had to have a go
She had them wi' her coffee, she even ate them on the bus
It's a guid job she was no' there a fortnight, I'm sure she would
    have burst

And Bobby went his dinger at the twin beds in his room
He says the castor on his bed once or twice let him doon
I ken one morning they woke us up, they had an awful carry on
Bobby was feeling amorous, but forgot he was accident prone
He tried to reach for Marion but misjudged the distance in between
He fell doon in between the beds, a rude awakening to his dream

And Alec fair enjoyed himsel' and he came in handy tae
He was always left to watch the bags and things, he was going to
    make us pay
But the holiday did him the power of good, and he never once was
    the worse for wear
He says he's going to gie up drinking, so as he can go back again
    next year

But time waits for no man, everything must come to pass
Our holiday was no exception, we had to make for home at last
So we decided to try and get seats together on our journey
    going hame
But alas things did'na work that way, things went haywire once again

Bobby's bag of duty free drinks went crash, he says
    Oh, no, bloody hell
But it turned oot it was'na all that bad, it was only Marion's muscadel
We'd to pour it oot his cigs and dear knows whit all mair
When he'd finished it looked as if he'd emptied his bladder
    on the runway then and there

Of course, that made us last on the plane wi' seats gie hard to find
Marion had the whole plane in an uproar before she'd sit
    on her behind
You see the only seat left vacant was between two gentlemen
She says, Dae I hae tae sit between they two folk I dinna even ken?

And once off the plane at Glasgow, we'd the customs to go through
Of the fourteen who went from Cauther, who was stopped?
   Of course, us two
Three times we've been a-wandering to lands away from hame
And three times we've been stopped at the customs, we're no' going
   back again

I would like to know what there is about us, that makes folk
   single us two oot
I doubt it's my gold fillings, I'll just hae to get them oot
But we've been hame sometime noo, and have had time to ponder
   and survey
The merits and demerits of a fantastic holiday

And I'm sure we'll still all be enjoying that holiday, many months
   and years from now
And thinking back on the many laughs we had, we'll enjoy it more
   somehow

1966

Working at the Co-op Bakery

I'm up in the morning, up with the lark
Since I started my wee job up at the dispatch
I'm no' long started, I'm learning the ropes
I like it all right, and daen fine, so I hope
The lassies I work beside are just like mysel'
We're mair enough the same age group
And get on very well

At the tap of the tree there is Nancy, of course
I hope I never hae tae dae her job for she has the most

Responsibility, frae how many pies, rolls and things
To how much bread yon Big Walter brings
But I must gie her credit where credit is due
She's as sharp as an eagle and her mistakes are but few

Then there's Nan – she does the Three Musketeers at the top
    of the bay
She fairly keeps them in order, they say
Again, so really, they're gie weel aff with Nan
And on Saturday mornings she helps by bringing oot Alex the heir
    to her clan
Then there's Winnie, or Winifred, if you like
She gets hurled in every morning with somebody
I don't know if it's by car or by bike

Anyway, she reminds me of a midwife delivering bairns
It's hoo she handles the half loafs, hoo she puts oot her arms
I've lost count of the half loafs she delivered
In the big bakery
But for handling yon eccentric machine
I think she deserves at least the O.B.E.

Then I'm called Bella, or I've seen me get Bell
I put the half loafs in the barrae and count them as well
Then I put the pies on the board, rolls and bridies an' a'
Everything is put up in rows, and I must say they look real braw

And I canna forget Mary, Krazy Kuts she's been assigned tae
She keeps looking ower her shoulder to see if big Tam is coming to
    take them away
She's that feared she'll no' hae them ready
Or that she's keeping him back
She says that she'll either go crazy hersel' or else get the sack

Then the van drivers come in, things hot up right away
It's, Nancy, hae you got an extra pan loaf or Slimcea the day?
Or, Whae's pinched my wee loafs, after I had them made up?
I'm counting, shouts Nancy, Will you kindly shut up?

It's really quite hectic at times, so it is
It's, Bella, eight dozen rolls for Betty and nine dozen for Liz
Or, Would somebody help me to lift this board of bread?
I run and I try to help but I drop it instead
Still, my intentions are good and apart frae the skelfs
I really dinna let many boards fall aff the shelf

I'd like to tell you about all the drivers
But I'll just single oot wan
He's really that popular, his first name is Stan

I hope he doesn't object to me singling him oot
But he's such a loveable character, like oot of a book
His patience amid life's trials and strifes
Would show us all an example on how to take life

And I would not like to leave oot Mrs McCallum
Wha gies oot our pay
To us all every week on silver Saturday
And whiles if we forget oor flasks or run oot of tea
She boils up the kettle and charges no fee

1965

Cauther Brass Band

I bet you're all sitting wondering just what I'm going to say
For an occasion such as a Centenary doesn't happen every day
I was asked to write a wee bit verse and telt tae try and make it guid
And if I required the minutes book I would get them from Mr Rigg

Well, to put it mildly, I would say, I was a wee bit taen aback
I had visions of the reverend gentleman in a band uniform and hat
He's plenty room to practise in yon muckle great big manse
And his Irish Setter, an uncomplaining audience

But let's go back a hundred years and learn a bit about the band
For, I'll have you know, at one time it was famed throughout the land
The first bandmaster, I am told, was an Alexander Ross
And in eighteen-sixty-eight, his son the first boy member was

In eighteen-ninety-seven with Dr Young as president
They formed the musical union and various bandmasters came
     and went
Then it became a public band in nineteen-twenty-six
And they reached the top of the charts in '38 – you'll all remember it

That was the year of the Empire Exhibition, they played there for
     a solid week
There's nae doubt in they days Cauther Band was hard to beat

Oh, they played all ower the country, even up at Oban Highland Games
And they've practised in all the halls in Cauther, even in
     band members' hames
It's also said at one night, while they practised in The Happy Land
Mrs Cowan gave birth to Agnes and disrupted Cauther Band

And they've even had the honour of playing in the Albert Hall
The test piece was called Freedom but their luck wisnae in at all
They didnae win any trophies that time and the only freedom
     that they had
Was when the thing was finished, Cauther Band had been gie glad

Another place they played at was Edinburgh Zoo
I hear they were very popular – and with the animals too
It's said, you know, at one point, a chimp grabbed yon wee stick
     in its hand
And had the crowd in stitches conducting Cauther Band

They drew the biggest crowds, they tell me, when Cauther Sports
     came round
At the band draw the night before turned oot
     the whole o' Cauther toon

The first ambulance in the district was raised by the brass band draw
And the Nursing Association was started wi' money raised by
them an' a'

There's lots of names connected wi' the band worthy of a bit o' praise
If I were to name them a' I'd be standing here for days
But there's nae doubt we're a' proud of them, Cauther Band has
served us well
They couldn't have done any better than Gabriel himsel'

I think we should all make more use o' Cauther Band
We could start by getting Kirk Brothers to build a new bandstand
They could play there on Sunday afternoons, just as they did in
days gone by
And who knows they might regain their fame, it does no harm to try

1967

A Day at the Races!

One Saturday morning Andra phoned up
He said we're goin' to the races to try out oor luck
I wondered if Bella and you would like to gang tae
We could hae oor dinner somewhere and just make it a day

You see, Andra had friends that were green keepers there
And we would get in for nothing, of that he was shuir
They had been there before and they kent a' the downs
You go in by the back door, and that way save a pound

Well, the races are a place I never had been
But I thought I would go, for you ken, so does the Queen
It would be quite an experience to see a racecourse
And I might win a wee fortune if I could pick the right horse

So we all started off, it was a bitter cauld day
It was the first day of April and there was snow on the way
When we arrived up at Kelso my legs were that numb
And I'll be truthful in saying, so was my bum

The first race was past by the time we got in
So we made for the paddock before the next race could begin
You see, they parade all the horses for you tae look ower
And make sure they've a head and a tail and legs no mair than four

You're supposed to pick one you fancy, the one of your choice
Note the vital statistics, its carriage and poise
Then they bring on the jockeys, aye they bring them on tae
You can pick your favourite colours, sometimes you've mair luck
    that way

I picked Southern Stranger in yellow and blue
And I stood and I shivered, my nose was blue too
It did no' sae bad, it came in third in the race
But they did'na pay oot for third, which I thought a disgrace

The next one I backed was called Mister Garter
I kinda fancied the tartan sash on his master
The next I picked oot was called Girl Guide
But I think they two were just oot for an afternoon ride

Then I picked oot a winner, Shady Wull was his name
He was a magnificent beast with a beautiful mane
I was up in the clouds when he actually won
I thought, Noo, Bella, your luck's just begun

But when I heard my profit was a mere one and ten
I felt like kicking the brute as I passed by its pen
Then I fancied a grey horse, this time one Billy Gray
But poor Billy fell, it just was'na his day

Then the last horse I fancied was called Hettie Bell
It ran about last, I could hae done better mysel'
And the fashions I saw, oh, you should have seen this
If I had worn yon in Cauther, it would hae caused quite a tizz
Trouser suits as they call them, bright orange and green
And dresses that left an awful lot to be seen

And, of course, to round the day off we had tae have something to eat
We thought a slap-up dinner would make it complete
So we went to a posh place, The Cross Keys it was cried
We had started oor soup when of shame I nearly died

For Andra shouts to the waiter in his ain special way
Hey you! What about some bread for my soup and Michael wants
 some for his tae
The waiter came ower, he was foreign, I think
He put some rolls on the table and Andra gied a bit wink

Where are you frae? You don't belong around here
He replied, Your dialect I don't understand, sir, I fear
We finished oor dinner without much mair a-do
You never weary with Andra, that's true

But I enjoyed my day at the races, I would go back again
And I would see next time I was clad for the snow and the rain
I would put on my trousers and borrow a big duffle coat
And I would put my money on wi' a bookie and no' wi' the tote

April 1967

Harburn Clubhouse – Two

To the tune of 'A Gordon for Me'

We're taking up the golfing, we're learning up here
With an instructor and caddy, we've nothing to fear
You'll nae doubt hae noticed, bang in fashion are we
Now the first step in golf, you start off with your tee

CHORUS

The golfing for me, the golfing for me
There's nae place like Harburn, I'm sure you'll agree

Michael Kirk Jnr

St. Andrews is braw, Gleneagles an' a'
But the Club up at Hardale's the best of them a'

But we're keen to get started, we play by the rules
And though we might look it, don't think we are fools
We start off by shouting, Is it three? No, it's five
And watch our wee ball as it runs up the drive

CHORUS

We must watch our stance and also our swing
Or we'll find to our horror, we've missed the damn thing
We hook it and slice it and dear knows what a'
It's amazing the things you can dae with a ba'

CHORUS

Alec Meikle's Birthday

Dear Alec, just a few lines to say
Many happy returns of the day
You're aye in hot water, but you canna help that
And if you let doon on your calories, you might lose some fat

But as this is a new year starting for you
We hope you'll make a bigger effort to see other folks' point of view
And be kind to your ma, remember her age
Don't flee off the handle and get into a rage

Think of your blood pressure, it could dae you harm
You're needed a while yet, to look after the farm
And Andra and Bob aye need your advice
On how to rear pigs and get a good price

And that wee disagreement over Fiona's fur coat
You'll just need to let her wear it, noo that it's bought
You canna get your ain way every time, I'm shair
And Fiona disna object to the things that you wear

For instance on Sunday, at Parkhead when you call in
You should wear your guid suit and polish your shin
Don't wear your wellies and auld dungarees
They're all right for Gavieside, but Alec, oh, please

Think of Fiona's grand neighbours, what must they think?
Apart frae what you look like, just think of the stink
And Alec for your birthday, I think you must get
A new seat for the ditcher, so as your wee bum disna get checked

For what would Bob Lorimer say if he was called oot to attend
And put a coolin' poultice on for his boozing friend
It might be embarrassing and you could'na sit doon
Just think of the talk if that got roon the toon

But, dear Alec, we ken you take this in jest
You're no' a bad sort, you're one of the best
We all just thought we couldna let your birthday go by
You're just one lovely fellow, you're a wonderful guy
Happy birthday, dear Alec, from all us daft folk
You get younger each year, just like auld Jock

November 1968

Reply to the Lassies

It seems it is my duty the toast to the lassies to reply
Well, I've never done this before but I am quite prepared to try
Thank you, Bob, for all you've said in favour of the lassies
But noo I'd like to say a word before this evening passes
I don't know where you've got your facts or if it's just imagination
But I think that for a bachelor, you've got a lot o' information

But this business o' the pent and pouther, noo, Bob I'd like to say
If you'd only but tell the truth you wouldna hae us any other way
And while we're on the subject, you men are just the same
With your hair oil and your aftershave,
Aye, noo two can play that game

And then there is the mini skirt, I think we played right up their street
We ken they've got a rovin' eye and it's no' wasted on our feet
But if Rabbie he were here today, I'm sure he would agree
You men are awfy lucky that can glimpse a lassie's knees

But don't think I'm going to let you off
You've some gie queer fashion tae
Especially the younger males that are goin' aboot the day
They wear the hipsters, as they call them, they come to about there
In fact, if they were any shorter, it would leave a lot gie bare

But I dare say we're all much the same under all our fancy gear
We'll no' hae changed much really
We'll hae been the same throughout the years
But we lassies aye hae had a soft spot kept especially for you laddies
The auld yins, the young yins, the bachelors and daddies

Aye, we've seen a lot of changes and there'll be a lot to come
But I must admit without you laddies we'd hae missed a lot of fun
So, ladies, be upstanding and drink a toast wi' me
Here's a health tae a' oor laddies, at hame an' ower the sea

Sandy Lorimer

Sandy's five and at school noo, learning to read and write
He goes off each morning all spruced up
And comes back looking a sight

His socks are doon round his ankles
His blazer and bag hanging off
His school cap's all squeegee
And you cannae help but laugh

His shirt tail's hanging out, but he doesnae care
And when he looks for his mittens, there's only one there

He thinks he had them both on
When he came oot of the schule
But then he thinks maybe he didnae
It could be there still

Then he changes his mind
He had them both on when he left the class
And he came roon by Tennants
With wee Peter Brash

And dae ye ken whit's in the window, Bella, says he
A lovely big crane, it would just dae for me

I telt the bold Sandy to get back doon the road that he came
And try and find yer mitten before yer mammy gets hame
Go on noo, and hurry and see if it is still there
I cannae be bothered, says he and I've got another blue pair

But back to the mitten, it was made of sheep skin
They were no' long new, and one was nae use to him
So I went back doon the road to help him look for his mitt
But Sandy's mind just wisnae on it
It was still on the crane, and just like a lad
He wondered if he could get it if he talked to his dad

Then oot of the blue he decided to call off the hunt
I want a piece on syrup, says he with a grunt
Anyway, I'm cold and I just want to go hame
Somebody'll find it in the morn
My mammy's sewed on my name

I thought he was right
And seeing there was nae sign of the mitt
You ken when you're looking for something
You never find it

We would give up the search
It was no' worth our while
When suddenly he spied it lying away down Kirk Style
I've got it, he shouts, with one of his grins
If we hurry, we'll be hame before Playschool begins

Aye, I can see Sandy yet
With his piece in front of the TV
I could write a book on all the things that happened
Between him and me

Tammy Woods – Annual Do at Meadowhead

Tammy owns a garage at the bottom of the street
I collected for the Gala Day at his place every week
He's very kind and helps us in every way he can
In return, he's got my custom, I buy oil there for my pram

Now, Danny and me are working folk, we don't own a motor car
And we've never been to Majorca and Switzerland or fields very far
But some day we might win The Pools, a really big amount
And will call in for our petrol in our new Vauxhall Viscount

Now Tammy's a man of independent means, he doesna need
   to work himsel'
He can ha' a game of golf any time knowing all is well
He also likes his coffee, he's in the café every day
But, och, he's no' the only one, I go in there for mine tae

Now, he was a rally driver, and a rider racing round the track
And Wull Bryce gave him lectures hoo to keep doon round the back
It's true he's had his fingers in an awful lot of pies
Or if he's no', Jock Hutton has been telling Bella a lot of blooming lies

Now Tammy has an awful lot of irons in the fire
He never lets the grass grow long, he's a man you must admire
I hear at one time he was doing three jobs all at once
I wonder how in the world he found time for romance

I hear he was once a miner, he worked in Blinky pit
Wull White and Johnny Fowler will bear me oot in it
He was awful keen to learn the drums and I will have you know
He was always playing knick-knack on the hutches doon below

Tammy Woods with Rena and Bella – The Alexander Sisters

He also did his duty and served in the home guard
In the days when things were rationed and he spread his piece
    with lard
And noo things are very different, for he's in the upper class
In fact, noo he's so well off, he has to pay so much surtax

Now, Tammy, we hoped you've enjoyed our wee duet to you
You did us both an honour inviting us to your annual how-do-you-do
We also have enjoyed ourselves, so thank you once again
It's a pleasure to do something for such a prosperous gentleman

Mary & Allan Maclaughlan's Wedding Day

Once upon a time there was a very bonnie lass
Who fell in love with a handsome lad while they were still in class
They really were quite young and people said I fear
This is just a case of puppy love, it will never last a year

But Mary and Allan stuck together, through as we say, thick and thin
And it became more apparent she was very much in love with him
So although they're still considered young, they've at long last got
    their way
Their fairytale romance came true, they've just been wed today

Mary's now a member of the clan Maclaughlan
So after nineteen years we're proud to say, a son for May and Tam
I looked up the Maclaughlan motto to see just what it was
Of course it had to be in Latin, it was Fortes et Fidus
The dictionary says it means Strength and Faith so I'm sure
    you'll all agree
Allan's bound to come up to standard with that kind of pedigree

Now, while we're on the subject, I somehow now recall
Tam and May had their wedding here in this very hall
They looked every bit as handsome as those two standing there
The only difference I would say was the colour of their hair

If Allan's as good to Mary as Tam has been to May
She'll be awful, awful lucky, and she will be, I would say
For I also ken his parents, and if this two turn out the same
They'll keep the kettle boilin', for they'll fill the hoose wi' weans

I ken the pair o' them being shy, had a quieter how-d'you-do in mind
But we're awful glad the way things turned out
And they've had a wedding that's just our kind

There's been an awful lot of weddings held up here in Harburn Hall
And it's up to us to make this one the happiest of them all
I know Allan and Mary will get on well
And wish them health and happiness and all they'd wish themselves

25 January 1969

ALLAN &
MARY.

Harburn Clubhouse – Three

There's another side to golfing, the wives will back me up on this
Sometimes it can be quite a strain upon our married bliss
They go up for a round of golf, promising to be back in time for tea
But you can bet your boots they'll be back between twelve o'clock
    and three

They're sitting up at the Clubhouse, playing dominos and darts
They never even gie a thought about going home to their sweethearts
Of course, by that time the women are all wound up, their main
    springs kinda tight
They're sitting there fair boiling and ready for a fight

Aye, it's no' that when it's our night oot, it's a different story then
But all we get is, Haud your wheesht – it's different when it's men
Oh, I meant to be home early, but things didnae work that way
Roy says, What about another round? I was sort of forced to stay

You pair should take your bed up there, and bide there a' the gither
If I had only had the sense, and listened to my mither
Keep your mother oot of this, she would'na ken a bisom from a club
No wonder that your old man is never oot the pub

You'll no' complain on Saturday, when it's oor annual Christmas do
And it's no' this when you're at me you're needing something new
You ken I'm all right up at Harburn, you can be sure of that
And here I am, I'm hame at last, at least I aye come back

Camping with Betty & Frank Ritchie at Oban

The Kirks and the Ritchies decided to go camping this year
And we settled for Oban, then got out our gear
We found an ideal site up at Gallanachmore
We pitched our wee tent and the Ritchies' next door

And some of the tents, when we had time to look roon
Were the very last word, and had two or three rooms
They had windows and zips, that seemed to be all the trend
While ours, more or less, were just wee single ends

Aye, they wer'na as posh but they kept oot the rain
We were really quite cosy, it was almost like hame
And we had all the essentials except a W.C
But we'd a wee plastic pail when we wanted to pee

Now camping to us was no new adventure
But for Betty and Frank, it was their first venture
Of life in the open and all that it brings
You ken, lovely fresh air and midges and things!

We all had a sleeping bag, plus a camp bed
It was the first time they'd been parted frae the night they were wed
But a complete change was what we'd all planned
And if they felt lonely, they could always hold hands

In the morning it was the Ritchies that were always up first
I think they must have been lighter sleepers than us
But Frank, I will say, is a first class cook
He can fry ham and eggs and still read his book

We all had our chores, though, we all did our bit
And when we were finished, we'd have a wee sit
We'd gaze at the scenery and discuss where we would go
Whether we would go hiking or sunbathe then go to a show

Oh, we had a great time, sightseeing, the lot
And every night we'd go somewhere and hae a wee tot
The only deterrent was the long twisted road back
With the water beside us, plus, the fact, by this time it was dark

But we always got there, trust Michael and Frank
Although at times the guy ropes were a menace and so was the bank
We had many a laugh before we settled down for the night
And there were some gie queer shadows on the tent when we
    forgot to put out the light

And, of course, for once the weather was simply divine
It's a true saying the sun on the righteous doth shine
All too soon the holiday was over, it was time to go hame
Back to auld claes and porridge, back to Cauther again

It did us all good, though, Betty's cough and her sty are away
And it's the first time Frank's stomach has behaved, so he says
And Michael forgot all his worries and shed all his cares
He was looking years younger, in spite of his grey hair

And, Bella, well, she'll tell you hersel'
A tinker's life seems to suit her quite well
Aye, there's something to be said for life in a tent
We fairly enjoyed it, we're fair glad we went

1969

Meals On Wheels

Perhaps you've seen a wee grey van wi' a board up either side
Driving aboot and maybe stopping near where some of you folk
    might bide
It's a voluntary organisation, they call it Meals On Wheels
They supply a nice hot dinner to folk that bide theirsel'
And feel noo they're getting on in years
To make a dinner is o'er much bother
Or folks that's no' sae able and there are quite a few in Cauther

So along with a good few others, mostly housewives like masel'
Though men are no' excluded, we've two or three of them as well
But they nearly always stick to driving
While we humble housewives serve
A hot dinner to the old folk and make sure they didnae starve

They soon all get to ken us
And they've aye something for to say
Like, Well, ma hen, what have you got for my dinner this cold day?
Or, What's your name, I've clean forgot. My memory's awful bad
Och aye, it's Bella, so-an'-so. Aye, I kent your mum and dad

And one old wife she always says we're angels in disguise
And declares it must her birthday be everytime she gets steak pie
And another always says to us that's another jewel in your croon
For giving up your leisure time to bring our dinner roon
And yin old man I called upon says, We're all that grateful, lass
And this shilling that I'm giving you would hardly pay the gas

We get to ken all about their families
And hoo weel they've a' done for themselves
And of course we get their wee bit grievances
Och, but it does them guid to tell
And once or twice when we spilled the soup and made their
    dinner late
You should hae heard the row we got, We've no' all day to wait

But ye ken, it takes all kinds to make a world, they say
And they auld folk have worked gie hard and served us in their day
So now it's up to us to do our bit and when they're no' sae weel
Make sure they get their dinner
Three cheers for Meals On Wheels!

The Reverend Wee Davie – D.K. Robertson

To the tune of 'If it wasna for yer wellies'

Polbeth has a grand wee church, bang right up tae date
Packed oot on a Sunday, in a queue you've got tae wait
Plenty willing helpers, tae pass aroon the plate
And the minister is the Reverend Wee Davie

CHORUS

If it wasna for Wee Davie what would we dae?
Nae Café or wee shop on a Wednesday
Nae Sunday lunches before we go away
If it wasna for the Reverend Wee Davie

It's a plain and humble building for ordinary folks
Everyone's on christian names Betty, Jean and Jock
You don't hae tae dress you can wear jeans or just a petticoat
It makes nae difference tae the Reverend Wee Davie

They've got their ain private army The Polbeth Volunteers
Some deserve a medal – they've been in it for years and years
Their battledress an apron, weapons are wooden spoons tae steer
And the commander is Ann the Reverend's Good Lady

Their regimental duties include washing dishes and scrubbing floors
They've also got a very famous elite Catering Corps
Joe, I think's the Sergeant Major, sells his marmalade at doors
Mair profits for the Reverend Wee Davie

They have yoga and keep fit and a play group for the weans
At a dry and cosy meeting place oot the weather if it rains
You can blether wi' your neighbours an' discuss your aches and pains
And confession if you want wi' the Reverend Wee Davie

There's the handicapped club on a Tuesday, the older men meet
    every day
Alcoholics Anonymous tae help keep you on the straight
    and narrow way
You can ca' the minister at any time, be it night or day
You can depend on the Reverend Wee Davie

You can get mairrit at any time, even on Sundays it's allowed
Bring the wean back later in its white shawl wrapped around
He'll be admired by everyone and you'll be really proud
As he's christened by the Reverend Wee Davie

They've got just what you're looking for in their wee Thrift Shop
If you need a bed or sideboard he'll see if he's got one in stock
He's getting mair like Harold Steptoe, he's looking for a horse
    and float
He's very enterprising is the Reverend Wee Davie

Yes, Polbeth Church is wonderful, it's absolutely grand
You can even rest a while in peace there before you leave
    this green and pleasant land
You'll get a fitting send off, and if you want you'll get the Sally Band
 Just leave it to the Reverend Wee Davie

1970

John Rankine's Birthday – The Florist

Dear John, this card is to say
Many Happy Returns of the day
We felt this special occasion we just couldna' miss
With a wave of the hand or even a kiss

We think that tonight, someone as nice as yourself
Shouldn't be left on his own, like a plate on the shelf
So forget about orders, and tatties and things
Let yourself go, never mind what tomorrow might bring

Don't think o' the shop, or that waddin' next week
Or hoo many hours you've been on yer feet
Don't let yer mind drift towards syboes or peas
Apples and oranges, or any of these

Forget about prices, we a' ken it's nae joke
Don't even think of the price o' Jessie's last frock
Or if the lassies are needing new shoes
Put it oot o' your mind, enjoy your freens an' your booze

And to the deil wha ever said, Say it with flowers
These last bouquets you made, taen hoo many hours?
And they folk that come in wanting your expert advice
On hoo to rid their roses o' greenfly, or even the wife

Tell them a' in your thoughts jist where to go
They'll no' be ony the wiser, but you'll feel better, I know
And a wee word o' advice on the subject of Alex's new car
I hope the price of insuring it
Didna put your blood pressure up ower far

Just go on your holidays, let it settle doon
Relax wi' Jessie and the weans in that wee hoose in Troon
The sun will, I'm sure, shine especially for you
There'll be nae clouds in sight, just skies o' blue

Put that shop in the main street right oot o' yer mind
Get away frae it a', leave your worries behind
P.S: Anyway John, the gist of this rhyme
Is enjoy yourself, Happy Birthday, have a wonderful time

Oor Dug

Last year we went to Holland for a holiday
And when we arrived back hame, our auld dug had passed away
I kent it was getting on and syne wid hae to dee
I vowed that when that happened there wid be nae mair dugs for me

Fourteen years we had Midge, when all the weans were young
It was like one of the family and gave us a lot of fun
So I put away its bowl and basket, now it was deceased
For I'm the kind keeps all sorts of things, and it wouldna eat a piece

I must admit the hoose felt awful funny, even the auld cat was lost
But I wasna hain' another dug, I said till I was hoarse

Then 'roon came our Silver Wedding, and seeing Tam Kirk was oor
    best man
I went up to invite him and May, and tell them all oor plans
Of course, Alice and Isabel had to come, they kent they aye had pups
They were only wantin' to see them, and were just goin' to chum
    me up

Well, we got tae Parkhead, and I guid them a' the jen
When the scullery door opened, and whit dae ye think came ben
A wee light coloured cairn pup, about five weeks or so
Alice looked at me across the room, her wee face a' aglow

Tam says, I hear you lost your auld dug, puir old crateur tae
You'll fairly miss her roon the hoose. Aye ye will indeed, says May
And hae you got another one? You've aye had a dug for years
For if you've no', I'll sell you this one, this wee tottie here

Alice said, Oh, Ma, goin' let's get it, my faither widnae mind
In fact, he telt us for tae get yin and this one's the very kind
So needless to say, we got it, we tain it there and then
It was a bonnie wee pup, but it wid'na tell us when

It did it on the carpet or anywhere at a'
It just widnae take a telling frae its faither and its maw
It chewed two pairs of slippers, the lining of oor John's suit
The arms of my three-piece suite, and a dictionary and library book

It even ate the legs of my glasses, they cost thirty shillings to renew
I shut it in the garage and it nearly chewed it through
I might also add when I tain it oot the garage, I left its basket in
And when Michael put the car away, there was an awful din
What in the name of God is that? He angrily exclaimed
Gets oot to see whit he's run ower, views the dog bed, or what
    remains

Then it comes into heat, a very trying time
I was heart-roasted wi' its suitors, but I thought I was daen fine
Until wee Jackie came roon one day, the end of the second week
The pair of them were nae match for me, being young and fleet

They got oot the door and through a hole in the basket weave
And Jock Russell's Rusty nabbed it, without a by your leave

I widnae hae kent aboot it if our next door neighbour had'na rung
And said, Bella, your wee Heather, I'm afraid has jist been stung

I've just seen them oot my window, they're oot on my front lawn
And I'm sorry for to tell you her thingma-jig is gone
Well, Michael, he was furious, and had to take it to the vet
As we didna want half poodle, half dear knows what, an injection
    it had to get
An' I had to keep it in another three weeks, that was five weeks in a'
I must be saft or daft or baith, that the pup's still here at a'

But that was no' the finish, its hair went an' all fell oot
Another journey to the vet's to see whit this was all aboot
He gave us some tablets this time and explained to Michael and to me
That the injection it had gotten had knocked its hormones
    all squee-gee

It was no' even like a cairn, it was mair like Basil Brush
Like a street accident, says Andra, and takes a len of us

LASSIE & LADY

Well, I had the auld dug for fourteen years and never any bother
This one, only eight months old and worse than all the dugs
   in Cauther

At one point in the proceedings I thought I'd stood enough
I was going to gie it away for nothing, it and me were in the huff
However, this week it hasnae widdled once or done a number two
And its hair's beginning to grow again, it'll soon be guid as new

I think it's got the message, it's turned ower a new leaf
For it kent if it didna, it was going to come to grief
I'll no' forget the things it did while it was growing up
And if anything happens to this one, I'll never hae another pup

1972

Harburn Clubhouse – Four

Winter will soon be past again and Spring is roon the bend
This is Hardale's closing social, all good times must surely end
We've had many enjoyable nights up here, every one's a great success
But I think the Scots night had that wee bit extra something
Maist folk seemed to like it best

And I wid like to say a big thank-you to Paddy for being such a brick
He could'na hae been mair surprised at the Valentine's dance
   had I gied him a sudden kick
I ken I taen him unawares and maybe caused him a wee bit
   embarrassment
But he taen it like the man he is and he returned the compliment

But really, the social evenings seem to go with quite a swing
Good fun, good cheer, good company, in fact here, they've got
    everything
Of course, the Committee do their very best, to see that all is well
And it's really no' any fault of theirs if ye don't enjoy yerself

Yes, Hardale's very popular, ye must agree on that
It's one place that's definitely got Welcome on the mat
I've no' made my mind up yet whether to join the golf or no'
Maybe I'd be like Andra, or worse, you never know

Then again, I might excel myself, I can see the headlines noo
Bella gets a hole in one, that would be some how-d'you-do
Anyway, I wish them all the luck when the golfing season starts
The summer months will soon go in, and then we'll a' be back

To see who has won the McInally Cup and who has won The Spoon
The same old faces will a' be back, the time will soon wear roon
In the meantime, thanks to everyone who helps in any way
It's a' the willing workers that make Hardale what it is today

Bella & Michael's Silver Wedding in Harburn Hall

This is the story of twenty-five years
In the life of yours truly and the timber man here
Frae we took the first steps of matrimony
That eventually led us to where we are the day

It was in this very hall that we saw the light
And kent for each other, we were just right

And the bad winter we had in nineteen-forty-seven, mind
   the snow lasted till May
That's really whit made Michael name the big day

For he was that browned off, being snowed in way up The Whang
He says, I've cycled this road night and morning for ower lang
I'm no' putting up wi' another winter like this
And so we settled down to married bliss

And we started off with no' much at a'
For things were on dockets, and gie scarce an' a'
We'd a table, a kist, no' forgetting a bed
And instead of fitted carpets, we'd rag rugs instead

And we had two chairs and a couch of lovely green plush
Bought at Lanark Market for five pound especially for us
And Michael made a wee table, Jock Young still has it the day
Its four legs were bits of a bannister he'd been taking away

On it stood a wireless, we thought was just grand
We used to listen to it on a Sunday to Mantovani's band
Aye, looking back noo, I think that way was the best
You have much mair fun when you build your ain nest

The years slipped by, along came the weans
They made oor wee but and ben seem mair like a hame
There were plenty of laughs, and tae sometimes tears
For you canna expect the sun to shine all the twenty-five years

But we aye weathered the storm, and although I say it masel'
Taking everything into account, we got on very well
And when we built oor ain wee hoose, well, that was a dream
   come true
Although the family all said, Ma, nae mair rag rugs noo

But I've still got a few, up in the loft they are kept
And if I took a notion, I could bring them doon yet
And then there's a' the freens that we've made ower the years
I've been warned by Andra, I've no' tae make ony mair

For oor freens are their freens, it's like that you see
And they aye go to see them, when they come to see me
And the problems we get mixed up in through nae fault o' our ain
But somehow or other, I aye get the blame

But apart frae all that, we would just like to say
A' the freens have rallied together to make this a great day
We've been awfy lucky, they twenty-five years, we've never had
    cause for regret
And I'm sure we'll all hae another wee do up here some day
For we've an awful long road to go yet

19 September 1972

The Weans

For West Kirk Burns Night

Well, I've done this duty once or twice, but no' for a while I fear
But I must admit I enjoy a Burns night when it comes roon every year
I've heard the lassies toasted wi' monie a different swain
And after listening tae what Frank had to say, I'm awfy glad I came

He says it is a privilege, as likewise it is for me
And as for finding inspiration here tonight, on that I must agree
For it's true Rabbie was endowed wi' a great attraction for the lassies
Whether they be frae humble hames or came frae the upper classes

They were his inspiration of that there is nae dout
He first became aware of it while he worked wi' Annie Rankine
    at The Corn Stooks
My Love is Like a Red, Red Rose, or Green Grow the Rashes
These song'll live forever, as long as there's lads and lassies

It's true we women've changed a lot frae Rabbie Burns's day
But basically we're still the same, just as charming, I would say
And I don't think he would hae approved of women's lib –
    whatever that entails
I for one will no' be burning my bra, I'd be like a dug without a tail

And this business of us wielding power through oor femininity
Now, Frank, if you would only tell the truth, you wouldna hae us
    ony other way
And don't you think that just because I've left my teens behind
I fail to notice that all you men today have also changed

You dress in brighter colours noo as frae they did in Rabbie's time
And you've your deodorants and aftershave that smell of Old Spice
    and pine

But if Rabbie he were here the noo I'm sure he would agree
You all look very smart indeed and pleasing to the e'e

Aye, we've seen a lot of changes and there'll be a lot to come
But I must admit without you laddies we'd hae missed a lot of fun
So on behalf of all the lassies, here's a toast frae me
God bless all oor laddies at hame and ower the sea

1973

Jimmy & Margaret Rennie – Silver Wedding Anniversary

It's twenty-five years the noo frae Margaret an' Jimmy were wed
The leaves were just turning an' the rosehips were red
The harvest was in, the clocks set to go back
Just the right time, when things were a bit slack

The ideal time for a farmer tae wed
Wi' the bonus o' an extra hour in the bed
They were married in St. Michaels, the reception held in Lea Park
I was the best man, the youngest of the Mossend pedigree pack

Just fourteen I was, ma mither's pet lamb
Lookin' forrit tae getting ma ain way once Jimmy had gang
They honeymooned across in the Emerald Green Isle
When they got back I couldn't help notice Jimmy's big smile

They stayed doon in the Kirkgate before moving up by
Settled doon nicely tae mairrit life among the hens an' the kye

They've no' changed that much frae that day long ago
They're happy the gither, it just goes to show

They made the right choice when they mairrit lang syne
So here's a toast frae the best man, a bit older this time
Here's tae the next twenty-five years an' mony mair
Tae Margaret an' Jimmy, tonight's happy pair

Toast frae the best man

The Paper Chase

Now seeing this is The Vaults Social Club annual how-d'you-do
I'd like to take this opportunity and tell this tale to you
It's a bit o' a mystery really and it's still no' solved as up to noo
It's about the disappearing toilet rolls and Em has lost a few

All her regular customers when they went for...weel, you ken
Were most embarrassed when they had to shout, Hae you a news-
    paper haundy, Em?
She often wondered where they went to and although it's no'
    a serious affair
It's very inconvenient when you're sitting wi' your trousers doon
    to find there is nane there

She wondered if Jock Robinson takes them for to clean his trowel
Or if Tam Walker uses them all up when he's troubled with his bowels
Then maybe somebody might just like the colours – thae lovely
    blues and pinks
Or do they take them to throw on the football pitch – to tell
    the referee he stinks?

They've such a lot of uses forby flushing doon lavvy pans
I mean, Joe Beck might be using them to clean his oily hands
Anyway, she hopes you will excuse her if you're ever in that fix
She's going to put in all her old newspapers so as you can tear off a bit

Ye ken that paper's awfully scarce and since there micht be nane
So here's hoping nane o' ye will take offence and think that you're
    to blame

Jock Robinson –
Retiring Council Foreman Plasterer

You've all heard aboot Jock Tamson, and how we are all his bairns
But hae you heard aboot Jock Robinson, for this is worth of hearin'
He's supposed to retire in February but they've asked him to stay
    to May
He's foreman plasterer wi' the council – they must be gie hard up
    I'd say
Between him and Tam Walker – he's the plumber's mate
Hoo the council got stuck wi' they two
Well, I suppose that's what they would call fate

And his wife calls in daily at The Vaults to check on him, ye ken
She sits on her stool and has her hauf and parlez-vous wi' Em
Jock has his hauf and an export, then he goes and leaves May there
But he comes back again at five o'clock, oh, aye, he aye comes back
    for mair

In fact, if some night he did'na turn up it would be a right calamity
Em would be forced to call a meeting and send word up to May

There would be panic stations, wondering where he possibly
    could be
For it's weel kent he would never pass The Vaults and go
    straight hame for his tea

Oh, no, something would hae to be very wrong to keep Jock frae
    his dram
Like getting marooned on someone's roof or stuck in some wife's
    chimney can
But I'm only joking, really, he swept my lum for me last year
And you ken, Jock, it's needing swept again for Santa Claus'll soon
    be here

Well, we've got to hae our little joke especially at these kind of nights
And I think it's only fitting the retiring foreman plasterer should
    for once be in the limelight
So, Jock, forgive me for poking fun at you, someone's got to be in
    the line of fire
I hope you'll frequent The Vaults for many a year and all the best
    when you dae retire

18 October 1974

Masonic Burns Supper – Reply to the Lassies

Well, here I am back again, it daesna seem a year
Since we all enjoyed your company doon at Mid Cauther here
Only this time it's Mr Renwick who's had a chance to air his views
And I must say he's done gie weel, I must gie credit where it's due

It never fails to amuse me though – the things they find to criticise
They seem to ken every little detail I think they've X-ray eyes

But don't you think that just because I've left my teens behind
I fail to notice a' your antics, I'm quite observant, mind

I'll start off with the wee laddies, they can be proper little horrors
They break your windows, kick your doors and cause nae end
    of bother
Then take them a' frae twelve to fifteen years try and tell them
    anything
They think they've nothing else to learn, their education's duin

And frae fifteen upwards, they think they're the whole cheese
They get thairsel' a' spruced up, the lassies for to please
And he talks of being swindled, again I must protest
It's weel-kent goods a' fancy wrapped are no' always the best

All that glitters is not gold, they'll find that oot ere lang
Then when things don't come up to scratch, it's never them
    that's wrang
He spoke kindly of a' mothers though, as weel indeed he ought
For whae else would stand whit they stand, a wife? I bet you not

And again he says they're lured away by some mini-skirted Eve
By joves, I've yet to see it although that's what they would hae us
    a' believe
And as for you poor downtrodden men, that's never off the leash
If we even spier whaur you're gaun we're telt, Noo haud yer wheesht

Aye, it's true we women have changed a lot frae Rabbie Burns's day
But basically we're still the same, just as charming, I would say
So thanks for giving me this honour, the toast to the lassies to reply
And when I say this I mean it, I'm no' telling ony lies
Frae the bottom of ma heart, frae lassies auld an' young
We would be nae use without you lads, like an envelope without
    the gum

1968

John & Agnes Adamson – Ruby Wedding

When John Adamson and Agnes Barr decided tae get wed
Britain was at war, when in church their banns were read
Times were hard, oor country's fate
In a balance lightly swung
But Faith, Hope and Love were on their side
An' youth, for they were young

They got married in December, a Wednesday it was
They'll no' forget it easily, I'll tell you why because
A white wedding it was indeed
Frost an' snow lay a' ower the country side
When at Bonnington Hotel in Lanark
John made Agnes his bonnie bride

They made an impressive couple for John was six foot three
Agnes thought, would he fit intae their double bed, it being utility
In wartime things were awfy scarce
They'd claes coupons, ration books
Even silk stockings were hard to come by
Aunt Kate slipped and ripped her only pair, the stook!

The wedding cake was a cardboard box iced on the top, etcetera
It was used at many local weddings, less calories, ha, ha!
Responsible for that work of art
George Smith frae Carnwath
Aunt Kate's hubby, the local baker, a master at his craft

Best man, of course, was brother Jim, tae get John tae the church
    on time
While best maid was Lizzie Forrest, her and Agnes always got on fine
They'd tae wrap up weel, keep oot the cauld
Watch and no' land on their bum

T'was quite stormy that year nineteen-forty
And there was mair tae come

They started their honeymoon in Crawford in the usual way
May I add the snow lasted till the end of January
Nae electric blankets, or even electric light
Just their love tae keep them warm
On cauld and wintry nights

They started mairrit life at Southolm Farm next tae the railway line
One hundred and thirty acres, eight milking kye
Life, they thought, was fine
Along came the weans in course o' time
Two lassies and a lad
They were extremely happy and content wi' whit they had

They got through the war years, they're made of guid Scots' stock
John became an elder o' the Kirk, they've aye been guid-living folk
Then they up and moved tae the Swaithes
Roughly a mile away
Five hundred and twenty acres this time
Sheep and kye of Ayrshire pedigree

The family are a' noo mairrit, an' fendin for theirsel'
They've got strapping grandweans, aye, didn't they do well?
Noo John enjoys his bowling and his garden
And when market days come roon
He loves a chaff wi' a' his cronies
Aboot the gossip o' the toon

Agnes also loves her garden, it whiles the time away
Sewing circles, coffee mornings and the church activities
That way they both keep busy
And John still gets up at dawn

Helps milk the kye, he's a great old guy
He still keeps farming on

They must hae seen a lot o' changes, in the years they've been
    the gither
We couldnae hae picked a better pair for a faither and a mither
They learned us weel, we're prood o' them
And would like for them tae know
We wish them many more happy years
And that we all love them so

So happy Ruby Wedding day to Agnes and her Jo
We hope you have a lovely time and, well, you never know
You've many a mile tae travel yet
So mind you both keep weel
Enjoy your lovely memories the gither
In your comfy hame, Locheil

Written By Request of the family, 1980

Bella's Driving Lessons

Noo, if you'll all just gather roon and listen carefully
I'll tell you about my experiences learning tae drive a motor vehicle
    on Her Majesty's highway
I phoned up the BSM, to see if they'd an hour tae spare
Explained I knew nothing aboot motor cars
Except they got you frae here tae there
As it turned oot, he was a local chap, I kent him as a lad
He asked if I'd a provisional licence, and I replied I had

Anyway, it was a' arranged that evening on the phone
Little did he ken whit he was in for, agreeing to take me on
Some of you might think it's easy, but no' for the likes of me
I thought that I was past it at the age of fifty-three
First he introduced me tae the car, showed me its vital statistics
    so to speak
And said he'd take me up the Woolfords Road
Wednesday morning o' next week

Well, getting tae start and stop the car was lesson number one
And I can assure you, that was easier said than done
It stalled, it jumped, it shuddered, then set off wi' a jerk
My reflexes were at times too slow and other times too quick

But I graduated frae the Woolfords Road, doon by the Waterhoose
Wi' Ronnie sitting there beside me, trying ma confidence tae boost
We came to the crossroads at Bellsquarry, and he said I had right
    of way

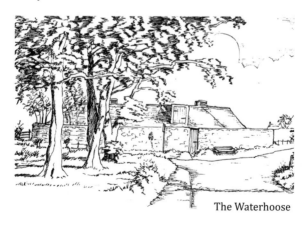

The Waterhoose

An' a lorry coming frae the left saw me an L driver and a woman tae
Thought, I'll hae time tae get roon before her, then whit did I go
an' dae?

I put ma foot doon on the accelerator, Ronnie put his hand on
the brake
We came tae a sudden stop wi' an almighty jolt, a guid job for both
oor sakes
I got an awful fright tae say the least, and I just thought, dearie me
I'll never make a driver, and so ended lesson number three

But nothing ventured, nothing gained, I continued once a week
And when I finally got the hang o' it, Ronnie taen me up the street
Doon tae Blackburn, then tae Bathgate, daein reverses, three point
turns, hill starts
Looking left and right and left again, there were times I quite
lost heart

And every night I went tae bed, I'd learn ma Highway Code
And hae a wee word wi' him up there, you could say a wee one
for the road
I'd often say, Do you think I'll make it?
Ronnie'd say, Aye, you're daein fine
Or I would'na be sittin' here beside ye, letting you drive this car
o' mine

Then came the day he thought I should apply to sit a driving test
It came by post, December twenty first, well, I could only dae my best
As it turned oot, it was market day, the car park was choc-a-block
And sitting in yon test centre was like sitting in the dock

Once we got oot he asked me tae read a number plate
Then we were on our way

I'd tae watch oot for folk wi' weans and parcels
It's no' fair I got that day

And when we turned the corner, the sun was low, shining in the sky
It really was blinding me, and I'm telling you no lie
I had tae take evasive action and I know you'll understand
There was nothing else I could dae, but drive only wi' my right hand

Well, soon it was all over, but you'll hae gathered all in vain
Then I thought like Bruce and the spider, I would hae tae try again

I got four wee x's on my form that day
One for no' acting at crossroads they thought properly
One for no' keeping tae the left while driving on the road
One for no proper use of steering wheel and no' looking left and right
    and left again, but I passed ma Highway Code

For two or three months I gave it up and had a rest, much needed
    after that
Then roon came Spring wi' all its signs o' new beginnings
And I thought, Time tae make another start
Then in August of the next year I sat another test
I got three x's on my form this time, at least it was one less
One for no proper use of signals and I failed reverse this time
Oh, aye, and no proper use of steering, but otherwise I did fine

Then I got a cancellation two months later, the same examiner an a'
This time it was pouring rain, I failed and I just thought, Oh naw!
I got one for no' meeting other vehicles safely, and no proper use
    of gears
It was always something different, ye ken I think the examiner
    was queer

Then I got ma man coaxed tae buy a wee old car, he wouldna let me
    in his yin
And my sister said she'd sit beside me, I was determined for tae win
I drove tae Woolco for ma messages, got tae ken Bathgate inside oot
Every minute I could get a co-driver, I took that wee car oot

So once again I sent away tae hae another go
It was Spring again and I had yon feeling a' rarin' for tae go
Ronnie phoned tae say his car was in the garage an hour before
    I sat ma test
Michael ran me doon in his one, noo, wait till ye hear the rest

My horoscope that morning said I was under planetary protection
    well I must hae been
For in Michael's car, I passed my test
I wouldna hae changed places wi' the Queen
It had taen me two years to make the grade
And each time I vowed t'would be the last
But I'd finally convinced the examiner I can safely drive at long last

I owe a lot to my instructor and freens who inspired me this fight
    to win
So there ends my little story on the joys of motoring
Since then Margaret and Jessie hae joined me, they've also got
    their degree
You can now add to the list of women drivers on the road –
    another three!

1981

Auld School Photo

I was sittin' in the hoose the other day, there was a lot I could
    hae done
But I was in yon mood, you ken, couldn't be bothered
    daen anything
So I thought I'd get my pencil oot and write a wee bit tale
Sitting at the fireside, nice and cosy, away from cauld winter's gales

Noo, whit could I write aboot? It would hae to be based on fact
And as I had come across my old school photo
I thought, I'll try something aroon that
Mind you, it's gie weel faded, age is bad for that, you ken
And we all look that young and innocent
A', well, noo where's ma pen?

I had a look at all the faces and wondered
Where are they all the noo?
Hoped life had been no' that bad for them
Had all their dreams come true?
At least there were plenty o' jobs in those days
Oor young folk were all called up
You left the school on Friday, and by Monday had started work

Myself, I went into service at the big hoose
Joined the Upstairs-Downstairs set
Maybe some of you ladies in the audience will have worn the wee
    cap and apron too, I bet
You got a half-day on a Wednesday and every Sunday off
And you got to ken hoo the other half lives, working for the toffs

Of course, some o' these laddies joined the Armed Forces later on
Right braw they looked tae, when in uniform
See that tallest laddie in the back row, the last I heard of him
He was working oot in tax-free Abu Dhabi
Where drinking alcohol is a sin

And that laddie standing next to him, they were aye a pair
His faither had a wee barber's shop, noo he's cutting and styling hair
Aye, laddies have their hair cut and blow-dried noo and permed
     if they feel inclined
Nae short back and sides nooadays but it's a more costly business
     mind

That laddie wae the wavy hair, Don Juan of the class
A' us lassies had a crush on him, but at that age it didna last
That one and only coloured laddie, his name was Kubla Khan
I heard he joined the Navy, that way he'd see his parents' far-off land

These two lassies in the second row, I thought they aye had brains
But they ended up just like masel', mairrit wae a hoose full o' weans
There was nae pill in these days, you had to take what comes
And by the time you found out what was causing it the damage
     it was done

That big buxom lassie joined the WLA when she came of age
She worked hard and did all right, she's a farmer's wife nooadays
Wae two or three cars in the garage, and a great big fancy hoose
A deep freeze filled to overflowing and every new-fangled gadget
     for her use

Oh, and she became a teacher, and she became a nurse
And that wee lassie wae the cheeky face

Became a conductress on a bus
They're a thing of the past, God bless them
You never see them ony mair
They're no' needed on the buses noo, the driver takes your fare

That good-looking lassie there, she became a GI bride
And went to live way oot in Texas, where the stars are big and bright
That red-headed laddie, and that other one an' a'
Went doon the pits, just like their dads, alas, one of them's awa'

And that laddie worked on his faither's farm
To be a dairy farmer was his aim
While that one there just could'na or would'na learn
He has a bookies shop noo o' his ain
And see him wae the glasses? The brainbox o' the class
He went to university, needless tae say, his exams he passed
He's a lawyer noo, so I'm told, one of great repute
I'll need to mind his name and number, in case I ever need bailed oot

They two lassies went to make munitions
The war effort was by then in full stride
When old Churchill was daen his damnedest, and we did it
Britain turned the tide
They three sittin' cross-legged in the front row on the mat
They were aye late for school, and you got the belt for that

Aye, the tawse was used quite frequently
And they can all say what they like
It never did you any harm, it helped to keep you right
And if you went hame greetin' tae your maw
You ken what you got telt
You must hae deserved it, or you would'na have got the belt

And just look at what we're wearing, did you ever see the like?
Short trousers and gym dresses, oh, God, don't we look a sight?
And there's the teacher and the Headie, he died years ago
And if the teacher's still aroon, she must be eighty years or so
She used to heat ma wee tin flask o' tea at the staff room fire
That was Red Hoose School before I went to Lyndsay High

That wee shy lassie wae the pigtails, I wonder who can she be
Oh, she mairrit a joiner frae up The Whang, help ma kilt, it's me!
I'd better move and get his supper, for every week I get the pay
Although he did'na go tae ma wee school, we met along life's way
Well, I've enjoyed reminiscing wae my old school photo
And I wonder if they too
Bring it oot frae time tae time and try and mind who's who

1982

Harburn SWRI – Sunset Glow – The Rehearsal

Good evening all and welcome, I know you've all come from
    near and far
And are sitting there anticipating what's in store for you wondering
    who's the leading star
Well, this is a new venture for Harburn Rural, we're very amateur
We'll no' win any Oscars, of that you can be sure

Now to put you in the picture, I'll tell you how this came aboot
It was Maggie who suggested it and the idea started taking root
Mrs Richardson was all in favour and agreed to help produce
    the show
We got a book out o' the library, chose a play and said we'll have a go

There were eleven women needed for the cast, so after a Rural
meeting one Monday night
We got all the characters all sorted out by picking folk we thought
were just the type
Oh, it was really quite hilarious, getting all licked into shape
And there were times I'm sure Mrs R felt like giving us a shake

Like the business of where and when to come on, also where
and when to leave
It was quite chaotic – it needed to be seen to be believed
And with a cast of eleven women, there was always two or three
couldn't make it
But you all know, the show must go on, we always found
someone else to take it

You all know the hall has been getting renovated, well, imagine
the upset
Yet faithfully on Wednesday evening the drama group still met

Harburn Hall

We'd to step over planks of wood and plaster board before we
    could reach the stage
Avoiding stacks of chairs and cardboard boxes, it was like getting
    through a maze

And some nights it was awfy cauld even with the Super-ser
The hall was really dismal – thick with stoor and awful bare
We'd to call in a local handyman with his hammer and his saw
To put an extension on the stage, it couldn't hold us a'

It made an awful difference, gave us more breathing space
And he built it all with six-by-two for you just never know – in case
And very slowly, week by week, we learned our cues and lines
Thinking some nights we were terrible and other nights just fine

Then we fixed a date, set the night of our gala performance
    you could say
While everyone rummaged here and there for props to get it
    underway
You'll have noticed all they wee nice extra touches, I'll no' mention
    any names
But a good few folk gave up their precious time and left things
    undone at hame

You must admit they're awful bonnie, quite a transformation
It just shows what can be done with a lot of time and patience
They say nothing ventured, nothing gained, we can but only try
Then wait and see what the critics say, once we get it by

So here we are all ready, about to start the show
I do hope you all enjoy it
Our first play – Sunset Glow

Harburn SWRI – The Performance

The ladies of Harburn Rural, I'll have you all know
Entered in the drama festival, their play Sunset Glow
It was our first venture into amateur dramatics, let me hasten to add
We put it on for our members and thought we did no' bad

They all said they enjoyed it and to take them at their word
If we entered they were sure we would come in about third
Considering there were only three entries, we said we'd gie it a try
And if we didna get third, we would want to know why

So we borrowed the flats, we'd nane o' our ain
Got oursels into Edinburgh, leaving husbands and weans
There were three or four carloads and a big transit van
Wee Jenny drove it as weel as could any man

Inside were the flats, props, couch, tables and chairs
Wae Joanna as navigator, there was no half-inch tae spare
Off went our contingent like an army convoy
Each following the other, my what a ploy

We'd tae be at Churchill, Wednesday night for half-past-nine
For a half hour's practice and get things into line
We were first on next evening at seven o'clock
So we'd nae time tae spare, we all worked non-stop

Then on came the fire prevention officer wae paper and pen
And said, Your chair covers and curtains are prone
Tae go up like a flash, just like a light
And there's a tear in your chair cover, it would'ne be right

But our producer, I think, must have turned on her charm
He agreed if we sewed up the tear, for the short while we might
    come tae nae harm
So we all breathed a sigh, you could say of relief
Thinking all that fuss over curtains, was beyond our belief

While doon in the basement in dressing room number three
There waited eleven budding actresses, ten others and me
For the play we had chosen had no more or no less
Than half of our members some nights at oor best

And we were all that nervous, it being the first time we'd been
Backstage, or on stage, if you ken whit I mean
Our make-up artist was busy applying lines here and there
While others were seeing tae this and tae that and taking great care
Tae see nothing was left oot, everything as it should be
Some getting that worked up they had tae run for a wee

Then came a knock on the door, time tae go on stage at last
Nae turning back noo, the die had been cast
We got through without major mishap, I'd say
Then we sat and enjoyed the other two plays

Then came the big moment, the adjudicator man
Stood up and told us to our face all we did wrang
It would seem our doors opened the wrong way and our chairs
    not suitably placed
He held quite a post mortem, but said in this case
We'd done awfully weel and hoped we'd enter again
I'll say this for the man, he left unturned nae stane

We got third as expected and we got a wee cup
And he said we'd a lot going for us, so that cheered us up
We were enjoying a bottle of plonk and a drop of the craitur
When who arrived at the door but the wife and the adjudicator
He couldna see us for reek, but, och, well, never mind
I expect he partakes of himself, tae help him unwind

He asked if we'd any questions or problems he wanted tae help
  if he could
Suggested we try a play wae no' such a big cast next time but he
  quite understood
It being oor first we'd tae see what a talent we had
And taking things into consideration, we'd done no' bad

So once again we got all loaded up in that big transit van
But getting out was a problem, Jenny didnae quite have the hang
She was hampered by rows of dustbins and it being dark
It was no mean feat, I assure you, getting oot that cul-de-sac

At one point in the proceedings, I thought Jenny's van had met
  its Waterloo
But somehow or other she managed tae squeeze it through
I was sure she taen off half the paintwork
But she assured us a' she taen off was a thick layer of dirt

It was quite an experience and we're awfully glad it's past
And although it was oor first attempt, it might no' be oor last

Davie Rennie's Toast tae the Lassies

It seems tonight, I've been singled oot this honour to perform
And to the lassies, bless them all, and the day that they were born
But, oh, I'd like to put you in the picture here
Although oor hoose was full o' weans
I never had a sister, and I didna ken yet what was to blame

So frae an early age, I lived in ignorance, the lassies didna exist at a'
This is wae the exception you'll hae gathered, of Mrs Rennie
    my dear ma
There was never any itsy-bitsy teeny things hung on oor washing line
Just rows o' flannel shirts and dungarees when the weather it was fine

Then school days came roon for me, it was quite a different story
There they were in all abundance, some plain, some awfy bonnie
Next came the teenage years, the best or so they say
When the chemical reaction worked overtime, both by night and day

It must hae been the same in Rabbie's time, the hazards were
    aye there
And his motto surely must hae been, he who wins is he who dares
For he dearly loved the lassies, he put them on a pedestal
They were like a glass o' wine to him and he surely had his fill

Noo in this day of unisex, male and female dress the same
Short hair, jeans, and woolly jumpers, I'm sure I'm no' alane
In thinking to tell the difference frae Wullie, Tam or May
About the only way to do it would be to hae a mass X-ray

I wonder hoo Rabbie would hae handled that, as he met them
Coming through the rye
I'm sure the result was bound to be many a black eye

Aye, and noo they've Women's Lib, they've burnt their bras
An' they're a' for equal rights
But still they've got that something needed
Tae make men rave about and write
They're no' only pretty faces, some hae brains as well
Some are awful clever-handed, I mairrit one masel'

We just could'na dae without them, wives, grannies, aunts, the lot
Withoot them, this old world of oors would come tae a full stop
So I'd like you to be upstanding while we drink this toast again
Tae the lassies, God bless them a', who make oor hoose a hame

Reply to Dave Rennie's Toast tae the Lassies

After listening to Davie, and whit he has tried to convey
There's naebody mair qualified to dae that toast than the milkman
    I would say
For he sees us in the morning, when we're hardly at oor best
A' newly-awakened, like wee birds frae the nest

Wi' auld dressing gown and slippers, hair a' in disarray
Withoot oor teeth and make-up, nae feminine frippery
And he says he missed oot on the lassies early by their absence
    dearie me
Auld Davie must hae got the Scotsman, so he also missed oot
    on Page Three

Ye ken a' yon lassies, sae perfectly endowed, their graceful curves
    displaying
Could dae a lot for ony growing lad, even set the old horse neighing
But living in the country had advantages

He soon learned about the bees and birds
Surrounded by God's creatures great and small, proving that time-
    less urge

As for Women's Lib and equal rights, noo, Davie, oh-la-la
I, for one, would fa' tae bits without my Playtex bra
As for this equality business, well, when all is said and done
There's naebody mair equal, than two halves joined as one

So we've no' changed that much really frae whit we were
    in Rabbie's day
We go through the same ups and doons and we're just as charming
    I would say
Our role in life, as before, is basically the same
An' you must admit, we all enjoy playing that age-old game

So, Davie, thank you once again
And I don't know whit you lassies think
But here's health to the male species o' our race
I hope they never become extinct

24 January 1983

Reply to the Lassies – West Kirk Church

Good evening, all, and thank you, sir, you I must congratulate
You've excelled yersel' the night at public speaking and noo you've
    taen yer seat
It's up tae me to air ma views this special Burns night
It's the done thing, one must reply, t'would only be polite

When Mrs Rankine first approached me to do the needful, I must say
I didna ken quite hoo tae go about it, I thought I'd got oot the way
It's no' an easy thing replying to someone you've only glimpsed
   occasionally in the kirk
It's different if you ken them personally and have an idea of what
   makes them tick
But I said I would make an effort and presume he's like the rest
Even though he's an elder and plays the organ
I hope he'll take what's said in jest

Now Mr Barclay implies a man admits to being weak when he
   agrees tae take a wife
Well, you know, I think without one, they'd be like forks without
   a knife
And to keep us as we've been accustomed to, well that's a matter
   of opinion
The way things are noo-a-days, wives are haen tae work
   it's happening tae millions
And he's trying tae make oot we're lazy, well, there's no' a man
   yet born
That would tackle a' a woman does, they'd say, Leave it tae the morn

And as for putting Playtex oot o' business, you can blame Erica
   for that
She fairly set the adrenaline flowing at last week's rugby match
They say she gave the English players the incentive to go on and win
She also gave the polis quite a handful when they went to run her in
But three cheers for oor polis, not an eyelid did they bat
They took care of Erica's statistics by whipping off their hats

But the majority o' us women will no' be discarding oors
We like to be well and truly anchored, an' anyway we're cowards
And we're into a' things, are we? Well, the reason is quite plain
The whole country was goin' tae rack and ruin until we took ower
   the reins

The reason we're in they positions, it's pure necessity
We've shown that we can do it, I bet you men never thought you'd
    see the day

Aye, we've even women elders, and they're also in pulpit garb
I wonder whit the reaction would hae been to that frae oor
    impulsive, self-forgetting bard
I don't think somehow he'd have adjusted easily tae the situation
And maybe it's just as well they were no' in vogue then
    kennin' Rabbie's reputation

But nae disrespect tae that great man, if he'd been at this
    how-d'you-do
He'd have said, I was born o'er early, the kirk's a lot mair human noo
But oor organist has the grace to admit without the ladies of the choir
He'd be like a farmer whose kye are at the grass
Wi' just an auld bull in the byre

But let me say in all sincerity, talking for present, future, past
Where wid we be without you gentlemen?
We'd be like ships without a mast
The day has no' quite come yet, when you can be done withoot
Just imagine a metal mickey asking if he could take us oot

No, we much prefer you as you are, from youth until old age
We're even prepared to make exceptions
When you're at the awkward age
So, thank you once again, sir, and I don't know whit you ither
    lassies think
But here's a health to the male species o' our race
I hope they never become extinct

January 1982

Be My Valentine

You all know about St Valentine and the lovely verses that he wrote
And Sunday being the fourteenth of February, suddenly I just thought
It would be an ideal opportunity for the first time in my life
To gie somebody a Valentine frae me, a middle-aged housewife

After all, there's nae set age for doing something daft
We could all benefit about this time by having a good laugh
But who would accept my Valentine and take it in good fun?
I wouldn't like tae offend anyone, I wonder could it be done?

It would hae tae be someone wi' qualities I admire
It's no' absolutely necessary he sets my heart on fire
For I'm quite satisfied wi' the good man that I've got
He puts up wi' a heck of a lot, there's no' much wrong wi' Michael
He's no' a bad sort

And I'm no' exactly Shakespeare, but never mind, who cares?
I think I'll go ahead and send one, I wonder if I dare

But let's get back tae thinking who will I gie it tae
I could gie it to Robert Rennie, but think what Ann might say
Of course, there's always Wullie Kirk, I could gie it to him
But Myra might get all uptight and chuck it in the bin

I could gie it tae Hughie Duncan, and happy would him make
Before he becomes a grandpa, dae ye think I'll be ower late?
Then there's always JR, noo, wi' a wee bit tact
A Valentine might be the thing tae penetrate his heart
And there's always David Steel, he's nice, if you overlook his faults
He kens me weel and understands that what counts is the thought

John Pearce

How about Andy Griffiths? Now, that would be fun
On second thoughts I'd better no', I'm old enough tae be his mum
I might present it tae Joe Meikle, he aye likes a laugh
Aye, there's nae swank about wee Joe, even though he is weel aff

And what dae ye say about Ian Gray? Now, that's worth a thought
No, I can imagine Maggie's answer
Too late, Bella, you've missed the boat

Do you think I should gie it to Allan Tuffs and set his heart aglow?
There's a certain air of mystery about someone you don't really know
But it might distract him wondering who could hae sent it. Who?
No, I don't want that on my conscience, he might run into the plough

It's getting to be quite a problem making up my mind
I think I'll close my eyes and throw a dart like Cupid, but I might
    hit somebody's behind
There's always Davie Rennie, I could ask him to be mine
But Margaret's my next door neighbour, I better no' step out of line

I thought of giving it to John Pearce
Now, there's a man that appeals tae me
And you never know, wi' a wee bit luck, he might get me on TV

Then again, there's Tommy Frame, he'd dae without a doubt
He's old enough and understands what life is all about
And Mary has a heart of gold, I don't think she'd object
But you never know, she might think, She's got a cheek, by heck

And there's Alan Douglas, I wonder what he'd say
No, that could be quite embarrassing, I see him every day
There's a dozen others I could mention but I bet you're all dying
    for to ken
Who I'm goin' to gie it to, oot o' all you handsome men
The suspense must be killing you, so before you all go hame
I'll put you oot your misery, I'll now reveal his name

He's tall, no' dark, but handsome, and he's going to be most surprised
But I think he'll take it in the spirit given
For he has a twinkle in his eye
So, sir, please accept my Valentine and make my dreams come true
There's something about a soldier
Colonel Leslie, it's for you

Harburn Hall, 12 February 1982

The Reverend D. K. Robertson – Bella's Sermon

I expect you'll a' be wondering just what I'm going to say
And I must admit, so was I up tae aboot a week ago today
Hoo on earth I got talked into this, I'll never really know
But Rev. D. K. can be persuasive when he likes
Saying, Go on, Bella, Have a go

You can tell them some o' your stories, I'm sure they'll go doon well
You've even got my permission
Tae tell the ane aboot masel'

I said, I don't think I've got the courage, in a church I'd never qualify
Ma stories might go doon well enough in Stewart Court
But I suppose you never know unless you try

An' you've got Effie Halliday participating, she's goin' tae oblige
Oh, well, I'll hae tae support us women
I can't let doon our side

I hope you realise ma kind o' humour needs a victim, in this case
    it'll be yoursel
I'm sure God understands, tae hae a laugh is very essential

So I'll get started on ma story in a style that's a' ma ain
Are you sitting comfortably?
Can you hear whit I am saying?

It's a' aboot the minister, the Reverend D. K.
Who at this very minute is doon in London
On his summer holiday

He aye goes doon tae London, he's been going there for years
There he can remain anonymous an' wear his latest trendy gear
While Ann often dreams o' a trip tae Paris or a wee sail up the Rhine
Something draws David back tae London
It's the summer sale at Harrods
They're aye on aboot this time

Morning coffee in the Fleur de Lys
Then off to his favourite corner in Hyde Park
He's whit I'd cry a professional people watcher
Quite an interesting past-time, could be quite hilarious, in fact

The Reverend D.K. Robertson

He visits a' the bookshops, an' Fortnum & Mason, he just loves
    tae mingle there
Has his afternoon tea an' cucumber sandwiches
They make sure he gets his ain special posh gold-gilt chair

He also faithfully attends the proms, he sits away up in the Gods
Wi' a' different nationalities, I wonder
Does he ever bump into the Lord?

I envy him the chance of hearing Pavarotti
The famous tenor, my, but whit a shame
He got drookit in the process
For did you see the rain? (And we a' ken who's tae blame!)

Soon before he kens it, his time's up, time tae get back to his flock
He usually comes hame wi' a lovely tan, some flashy ties an' shirts
    the lot
But sure as guns, he's nae sooner hame, he's back on his roons
    in that wee car
For he plays an active part in Neighbours, in fact he's the leading star

Noo, I'll take you back a few years, it's quite a long time
Would I be right in saying it was aroon fifty-nine?
A young minister, newly ordained, and new mairrit tae
Came to answer the call and show us the way

The first time I saw him, I remember it well
He's just a young laddie, I thought tae masel'
For ye wouldnae a kent by the claes that he wore
He was a man of the cloth, and I'll tell you what's more
He wasnae wearin' a dog collar, but a right flashy tie
And he had on a pink shirt, that's funny, thought I
Maybe he's no' the new minister at a'
Who is it beckoning tae me, fae ower the wa'?

Good morning, let me introduce masel', says he
I've no' had time yet, you folk tae see
I'm the new minister, David's ma name
Ann and I have moved into the Manse, our very first hame

I'll be ower tae visit you ane o' these days
But we belong tae the auld parish, quickly I says
That makes nae difference, he said wi' a smile
And that's been his policy, a' the long while

They're right guid workers, ye canna doubt that
He's certainly a doer, as a matter of fact
He helped dig the drains for oor hoose and creosote the beams
Naebody recognised him in his auld tee-shirt and jeans
And the comments he got frae passers by
Gaun hame frae the Legion, oh dear, oh my!

Then along came their family, Susie and Jane
Their school days noo ower, grown up like ma ain
An' the years brought their changes, auld Harwood nae mair
Nothing but memories o' the auld kirk that once stood up there

While oot here in Polbeth, a new church lives on
Doors open for business, no' just on a Sunday, but on every morn
For just as fashion dictates, the style o' claes that we wear
The church changed its style, that's what DKR's done oot here

Aid ever ready o' every description to whoever needs it
    regardless of rank
A band of workers, ready and willing to help where they're needed
    wantin' nae thanks

Playschool for the weans, a cafe, well run
You can get a three course meal, or just tea and a bun

The handicapped group on a Wednesday gaither
For a game of dominoes, or tea and a blether

There's a lot mair group activities, keep fit as well
And the church is packed on a Sunday, that speaks for itsel'
He administers tae a', whatever their need
As he once said, it makes nae difference, your colour or creed

Yes, it's quite a long time, he's been here a while
He still wears these flashy ties, he's no' changed his style
We've a' at some time, had reason to be grateful to him for coming
But aye bear in mind, behind every guid man, you'll find
    a guid woman

2 October 1985

Tam & Lena Rutherford – Diamond Wedding

Tam and Lena, as you a' know
Were married sixty years ago
They could show the young ones of today
That for life, married you were meant to stay
It does work, you'll a' agree
Just look at Tam and Lena and you'll see

They started off like most folk then
The bare essentials in a but an' ben
Nae carpets, washing machines or video
They were non-existent long ago

They lived their lives in Cauther West
And ower the years they built their nest
Like two love birds they duets sang
And they're still at it yet, Lena an' Tam

Tam started as an apprentice grocer wi' the Co-op
Where I masel' during the war my rations got
I mind it weel, ma auld store book
And the auld wooden box, where it got put
Then you waited till your name was called
Heard the latest gossip frae young and auld

Then your change it would come rattling roon
Along the tubes then wi' a plomp fa' doon
Aye, these were the days, were they no', Tam?
Weighing oot the butter, sugar, cheese and ham

Aye, and a' through the war years when the news was bad
And some mother's son got killed, puir lad
The whole grocery was filled with gloom
And we prayed silently, let it a' end soon

Auld mates Jock Hunter, Rab Muir, them a'
The weary wives, the trauchled maws
There's nae Co-op noo, nae divi-day
The supermarket's here to stay
Where folk go oot wi' trolleys piled sky-high
Wi' stuff we've never seen, or heard of, my, oh, my

And Lena was a cashier, also in the Co-op
Working in the office, up and down the stairs she'd trot
I think that's hoo she's kept sae trim, just look at her the day
She's like a young lassie still, even though her hair is grey

They're justly proud of their only son David, of Dr Rutherford
   I've heard tell
I've never ever met him, but didn't he do well!
They're also blessed with two lovely grandweans, a lassie and a lad
Haven't they been fortunate, life for them has been no' bad

They were among the first tae move into Stewart Court
They've been there from the start
Through life they've no' been just sleeping partners
They've both aye played an active part

Lena is a past president of WRI and sang in the church choir a' her life
Tam, of course, was in the male voice choir and sang duets
   wi' his wife
They're both weel-kent faces aroon Cauther
And we'd like tae wish them a' the best
So here's health tae Tam and Lena
And a married life that's stood the test

Letter to Mr Andra Graham

FRIENDS OF THE EARTH
BEECH TREE ROAD
13TH JULY 1985

Dear Mr Graham

It's been brought to our notice today you're fifty-nine
We Friends Of The Earth think it's now time
You took a rest from chopping down trees
We beeches and oaks request you to heed our pleas

The Waterhoose Road no more looks the same
Don't you agree that is so, Mr Graham?
Courting couples can no longer now
Carve their initials under our bough

Also, the British weather, when at its worst
There's no shelter now for anything caught in a cloud burst
This little beech, look, it's still very small
Won't give much protection at all
It might, of course, in about a century
But the folk around here won't see that day

Put yourself, if you can, in our place
What if someone were to decide you'd run your race?
They could say you're overgrown and overweight
The time now has come to exterminate

We've weighed it all up – the for and against
And since this is, they say, your first offence
We've decided to grant you a reprieve
No more chopping down trees, now, without a by-your-leave

Likewise, the fish and flowers of this earth
In future, please give them a much wider berth
God put them in trust, to me and to you
How sad if they were to disappear from all view

So, please, Mr Graham, you're not all that bad
Your past record shows you're a kind-hearted lad
Since it's your birthday, we'll go out of our way
And admonish you, sir. Have a nice day

A Friend Of The Earth

1985

Sixty-year-old Punk-Rockers

To the tune of 'Oh, Dear, What Can The Matter Be?'

Oh, dear, what can the matter be?
We're now over sixty and indulging in fantasy
We've kicked ower the traces, into gangs and graffiti
What do you think about that?

CHORUS

Oh, dear, what can the matter be?
We spray the bus shelters "Whae rules? It's yer granny!
What do you think about that?

Oor weans are a' up, nae mair responsibilities
We don't care for knitting or such frivolities
We discovered that life starts no' in the forties, but the sixties
What do you think about that?

For transport we've a bike, a Suzuki 250
We roar down the street, we're really quite nifty
The cops canny catch us, we canny half shift it
What do you think about that?

It's very exciting, also exhilarating
Gets oor adrenalin flowing, it's also breathtaking
Oor crash helmets are handy as a chanty or basin
What do you think about that?

Oor favourite pastime is going to the disco
And rock concerts we love and always say, Let's go
We're soon in the mood and doing the pogo
What do you think about that?

The hoose is a midden, we've nae time to red up
It's a thankless job anyway, we only get fed up
For meals, we aye buy things that only need het up
What do you think about that?

It's never too late to let it all happen
We just mug the teenagers if at us they're laughing
And when we're finished robbing a hoose, we aye let the cat in
What do you think about that?

We're really quite harmless, we just booster oor egos
Although some folk think we're a couple of weirdos
We hop on oor bikes and where I go, she goes
What do you think about that?

Who knows how long it'll take us to grow oot of this
We can't keep up the pace, it's just too strenuous
Oor spirits are willing but the flesh it refuses
And there's nothing we can do aboot that!

Anyone here who wants to buy a Suzuki?
We're gain back tae the big chair, telly, tea and a cookie
A wee game of bingo and the odd tutti-frutti
What do you think about that?

So, next time you see us, you'll no' recognise us
Two respectable grannies, no-one can chastise us
We're daen nae mair ton-ups on the by-passes
What do you think about that?!

Performed by Rena and Bella, 1986

The Sally Army

To the tune of 'Glory Glory Hallelujah'

We're here tonight at your request to help to save you all
For we all are sinners, there's no exceptions in the hall
There's still time if you come forward for you to see the light
So come forward please tonight

CHORUS

Glory, Glory, Hallelujah
Glory, Glory, Hallelujah
Glory, Glory, Hallelujah
Come forward and be saved

Your New Year resolutions have all went up in smoke
The cold winter's sapped oor energy and left us a' near broke
The fuel bills we've had tae pay has made us rant and rave
We're all needing tae be saved

Andra Graham fae Gavieside, come up and head the queue
We heard the Friends Of The Earth are most displeased wi' you
You hacked doon a' the hedges, the rules and regulations waived
Come forward and be saved

Big Wullie Russell o' Drumcross, we've a bone to pick wi' you
Control your beasts on the public highway, don't let them use it
    as a loo
In future keep your temper wi' the motorists, be true and strong
    and brave
Come forward and be saved

We've all lost oor patience sometimes, when we couldna see the light
The world's fair in a turmoil and wha's goin' tae put it right?
Reagan and Gaddafi, harsh tactics they've both used
Let's hope there's still time tae be saved

Maggie Thatcher, she is stubborn, some folk wid like tae see her
    get the boot
Like a woman she aye gets things her way, be it by hook or crook
Let's hope she manages tae keep oor heads above the waves
And pray we all might be saved

Mindful of our teachings have we gied a helping hand
To the elderly or housebound have we waved a magic wand
A smile or a cheery word that we have freely gave
All counts when you need saved

Do we really love our fellow men, their dogs and cats as well?
And treat them like the good book says, we would be treated oorsel'

If we try and keep the Ten Commandments be true and strong
and brave
Then we still might all be saved

So let's hope and pray that some day soon we'll have world peace
in our time
That the powers that be will see the light, and somehow
draw the line
Then future generations will once again sleep easy unperturbed
Join with us and spread the word

For Andra Graham's 60th Birthday

To the tune of 'Kissing in The Dark'

When Andra courted Jean, the world was quite a different place
An' folk as they get aulder, talk aboot the good auld days
The sun aye seemed tae shine then
The grass was aye green in the park
An' you could safely walk your lassie hame
An' kiss her in the dark

When they both got mairrit, things werena a' that dear
It was a shilling for a whisky and ninepence for a beer
Weddings meant a steak pie feed
And held when folk had finished a' their work
The best time of a', of course, was when
They kissed and cuddled in the dark

The purvey cost a princely sum of per person three-and-sevenpence
An' when they paid the honeymoon, his pocket felt the wrench

Thirty bob, two nights B&B, aye, it was all of that
Whit an awful price tae pay for kissin' in the dark

They werena that lang mairrit tae they had three weans in a row
Jean had tae put her fit doon, tell him tae turn roon an' sleep facing
    the wa'
Milkin' kye an' changing nappies were beginning tae leave their mark
Andra had got tae like it, this kissin' in the dark

They prospered an', I would say, climbed the ladder of success
Andra thinkin he was aye the boss, Jean let him think he was, oh, yes
It saved monie an argument, she never answered back
That is until, of course, she got him tae herself
When they cuddled in the dark

They both grew older gracefully, let things take their course
They didna let things get them doon, they never gied up the ghost
The colour of their hair has faded
An' they've both put on a bit of fat
But they're both still quite capable of kissin' in the dark

So the best of luck tae the pair of them fra' a' their family an' freens
They seem tae accumulate mair and mair, ower the forty years
    it seems
We're lookin forrit tae the year two thousand and two
When wi' a bit o' luck we'll be asked back
For there's nothing better tae keep you going
Than kissin' in the dark

Three cheers for Andra an' Jean, his bonnie wife
They've proved in this modern tapsalteerie world
That marriage still can be for life
Their recipe was an' still is an undisputed fact
Once they turn the light oot, they aye kiss an' cuddle in the dark

13 July 1986

Reply – Harburn Community Burns Supper

Now it's my turn to reply to the great JR
Whose memories of Harburn go back further than mine an' on
    a much higher par
His chosen profession kept him away for a number of years
Now like the emigrating bird, he's come back to this place
    he holds dear

The place where his roots are, among auld freens an' auld faces
His memory lingers on auld times an' auld places
He minds of the auld village school – I attended it masel'
    when I was wee
One teacher, Miss Beveridge, where I learned my A.B.C

Aye, and the railway station, now no longer in use
The Dobsons live there now, it's a nice family hoose
They had their ain policeman tae, wi' his sturdy auld bike
Tae help keep law and order, an' in wartime
See you warna showing a light

The shepherds and farmers and the gentry and a'
They'd tae abide by the rules, both great and sma'
And although JR was away quite a while
He kent a' the goings on aroon each homestead for miles

Now, looking around, what now does he see?
Harburn invaded wi' hordes of Englishmen, oh, dearie me!
We've names up here we've never heard o' before
Like Pearce and Tuffs, and an awful lot more

They've stirred Harburn up wi' their new-fangled ways
There's mair artists than farmers noo round its banks and braes
There's nothing they'll no' tackle, gie them their due
They're into a' kinds of things and lead busy lives too

They're a' freens o' the earth, just gie them a cause
They want things to remain as they were, according tae nature's laws
Ban the bomb, save the whale, the birds an' the bees
Pond life an' plant life, no' forgetting the hedges and trees

A' the new brood in the village, giving it a new lease o' life
Each helping the other, now isn't that nice?

The old hall once again has come into its ain
Within it they hold craft fairs, pantomimes an' playgroups
 for the weans

An' look at the changes in a' the big hooses a' roon aboot
Instead of the maids it's the mistress herself who cleans
 the rooms oot
You can even dine or bide up at Harburn big hoose, if you've got
 the right cash
For a wee while you're a member of the upper class

If they need a babysitter to let them oot on the spree
It's a case o' I'll watch your weans, and some night you can dae it
 for me
And if their car's in the garage, and to work they must go
They aye get the haud o' ane somewhere, they never say no
Wha's needing what, I'm goin' doon tae Cauther
It's like that a' roond, nothing's a bother

As one who has lived around here, and born along at Kiprig
Their motto up here must be, If I've got it, you've got it
That's hoo they live
Yes, the community spirit is very much to the fore
If you don't get what you're looking for at one place you just try
 the next door

Whether it be talent or time, or you just need the loan of a case
You'll aye get it up here, Harburn's a super wee place

February 1987

Chrissie & Wullie Brash – Ruby Wedding Anniversary

To the tune of 'Johnny Lad'

Wullie met a girl in Edinburgh many years ago
He met her in the Cavendish, as some of you may know
He thought, Hullo, hullo, hullo
I could dance the buckles off her shin, come on, Wullie boy, let's go

Noo, Wullie's footwork was a work of art
He used to play centre for the Hearts
He'd plenty practise wi' the boys playing football in the park
As he crossed the floor, as he crossed the floor
He thought, She can dance the buckles off ma shin
But I'll be back for more

Chrissie was an expert dancer, he soon found oot, by jings
She was made for dancing and did the can-can at the Kings
Aye, they were a pair, they were indeed a pair
They were like Fred Astaire and Ginger Rogers
As they danced aroon' the flair

Wullie tackled Chrissie like he did on the field the ba'
He manoeuvred her right brawly, a great match, said all who saw
An' he said, Wi' you Chrissie dear, wi' you
I'll dance the buckles aff your shin
If you'll say I do

The pair of them got mairrit, that was forty years ago
He brought her oot tae Cauther to a wee hoose in Hartwood Row
And that is where it started a' frae there
He said, Never mind the buckles on your shin
Come on, get up that stair

Wullie never played a better game, an' soon came goal Number One
Chrissie was the envy of all Hartwood Road as she pushed oot her
new son
Do you know why because, do you know why because
Ma wee pram was a Utility, her's was a Silver Cross

The Health Service had just started, everything was free
Cod liver oil an' orange juice, dried milk, so you can see
Soon came goal Number Two, then goal Number Three
Wullie hadna time tae dance the buckles aff her shin
For they'd weans on every knee

The hoose was filling rapidly, wee laddies everywhere
Chrissie says, Noo, Wullie, I'm no' haen any mair
For aye, wi' you, I can see wi' you
I could end up wi' a football team, you're suspended as from noo

But Wullie played another game once things had quietened doon
Goal Number Four, a lassie tae, they both were ower the moon
Aye, so you see, what will be will be
We'll dance the buckles aff oor shin, when they a' grow up, says he

Well, noo's the day and noo's the hour, they're a' grown up at last
Forty years have come and gone, just like a flash
An' wi' you and wi' you, wi' you, Chrissie, dear
I'll dance the buckles aff your shin, when I finish ma hauf and beer

Well, we're a' gathered here tonight to help them celebrate
Family freens an' neighbours, grandweans, something you canna bate
And frae me and frae you and you and you
We wish them long life and health and happiness tonight
And all their tomorrows too

1988

Supergran

You'll a' hae heard o' Supergran, there's mair than ane aboot
Some are tall an' skinny, some are wee and stoot
They're a bit like Santa Claus, popular wi' the weans
Though sometimes they get crabbit, and prone tae aches and pains

You find them in a' kinds of places, in fact they're everywhere
Some hae got false teeth an' glasses, an' some's got tinted hair
But they're always there when needed, baby-sitting an' the like
Watching the weans when they're off school, due tae the teachers'
    strike

You mostly find them aye at hame, beside a great big fire
Though it's no' unusual tae find them in the byre
And when the wean's got colic, and yelling fit tae bust
They bring them roon tae Granny's, tae pacify and nurse

We couldna dae without them, that's a weel known fact
They're even kent tae carry on, despite rheumatics in their back
They put on thermal underwear, of the weans they're very fond
They spread their pieces, tie their laces and wash their dirty hauns

They're awfy guid at sorting any squabbles that happen tae arise
For grannies hae experience, in fact they're very wise
They're forever patching trousers, putting zips in anoraks
And sometimes we lose oor patience when they fight
    like dogs and cats

They're awful guid at minding birthdays, they get plenty warning too
The weans aye tell us weeks in advance when their birthdays are due

They hint the back tyre on their bike is bald, and that's against
    the law
And the chain is no' working properly, it's awfy hard to ca'

And when they get tae teenagers, awe moody an' depressed
Complain their claes are oot o' date, and their hair's a mess
Well, grannies try tae boost them up, for we a' know full well
We've lived long enough and seen it a' before, aye, an' went through
    it oorsel'

What wid they dae without grannies? They tolerate the lot
They gie mair tae their grandweans than their ain yins ever got
Although they might seem auld, they were once young jist like them
So three cheers for the Supergrans, hip, hip, long may they reign!

1987

Santa Lost at the Waterhoose

CHORUS

Jingle Bells, Jingle Bells, Jingle all the way
Nae Waterhoose tae guid him, whit will Santa dae?
Jingle Bells, Jingle Bells, whit will he dae this year?
He'll like as no' go fleeing past thinking, My, that's queer!

For years and years and years, since eighteen-eighty-two
Santa's used the Waterhoose as a landmark, yes, that's true
Noo it's no' on the map, Santa's in a flap
Since he turned off the Milky Motorway
He's lost, and that's a fact

Harburn should be near, he draps doon into second gear
There's Auchengray and Cobbinshaw, the loch's right over there
He gies his reindeer a bit dig
We'll soon be passing ower Kiprig
My God, it's just a heap o' dung
There's neither stane nor twig

Whit's this we're passing noo? A brand new bungalow –
    but whose?
There's been some changes going on since last year, I'm telling you
I wonder if they've got any weans for on my list I've got nae
    new names
It's been put up fairly recently, they've got some view, a' the same

Whoa, Rudolph boy, whoa whoa, there's the finger post, oh, no
There's nothing there but a wooden bench, nae shelter
    frae the snow
Oh, it disnae look the same, I wonder who's tae blame
Where the devil's Harburn? We canna disappoint the weans

My, the place looks bare, Harburn should be around somewhere
We're running late, let's hurry up, there's no' much time to spare
I hope the Dobsons have swept their lum and Sandra's left some
    o' her black bun
I'm glad the journey's nearly over and we'll soon hae the job done

FINAL CHORUS

Jingle Bells, Jingle Bells, Jingle all the way
Santa made it up to Harburn in time for Christmas day
Jingle Bells, Jingle Bells as he tucks into his goose
He tells his little helpers aboot the missing Waterhoose

1985

Burns Night at The Hoose o' Collin

To the tune of 'Duncan Gray'

Duncan, at this time last year
Sat doon an' thought o-ho!
Let's hae a Burns Supper in the hoose
Margaret says, Yes, dear, why no!
We'll ask the neighbours roon aboot
Tell them get yer Burns songs looked oot
It could be quite a night without a doubt
It's a great idea, Duncan-o

We had, of course, the usual fare
Cockie-leekie, just the thing
Haggis, neeps, the lot, whisky, of course
Tae mak' them sing
Oatcakes, cheese an' dumplings tae
Candlelight tae show the way
Rabbie's photo, since he couldn't make it tae
A great idea, Duncan-o

We sang his praise in song an' verse
Some sang high an' some sang low
We a' had oor tartan gear
A great idea, Duncan-o
He did Holy Wullie tae a tee
Well fortified by barley bree
Everyone they did agree
It's a great idea, Duncan-o

John, he did excel hisel', toastin' the lassies
    ane an' a'
The reply was gaen by, let's see...
A Bella Kirk frae Ower the Wa'
The haggis was, of course, addressed
By Davie in his Highland dress
And as everyone they raised their glass
Said great idea, Duncan-o

Ian the tale o' Tam O' Shanter telt
Withoot a hitch he recited a'
An' some o' Rabbie's greatest songs
Were heard that night in Hartwood Row
Wullie's famous tenor voice
Gied us the love song o' his choice
Says Myra, an' her een were moist
A great idea, Duncan-o

Margaret frae across the road
Telt us aboot The Unco Guid
We'd a duet frae Michael an' Wullie tae
Everyone their wee bit did dae
An' as oor glasses they got trim
They were quickly filled up tae the brim
A great idea, Duncan-o

Some that were too shy thersels tae sing
Joined in the chorus, oh
My Love She's But A Lassie Yet
Green Grow the Rashes o
We sang A Man's a Man, O' A' the Airts
Scots Wha Hae, an' Ae Fond Kiss
There wasna many songs we missed
A great idea, Duncan-o

Instead of fiddling intae the wee sma' hours
It was a guitar and moothies-o
That was a' the musicians we had
The mair they drank, put them in great fettle-o
Ann and John practiced for days
On a duet Ye Banks an' Braes
The talent that night had us a' amazed
A great idea, Duncan-o

We were there until the dawn
A great time was had by a'
Rabbie's silhouette seemed tae come tae life
As the cock began tae craw
We ca'd it a day an' made for hame
Singing, yes, We Will Came back Again
Leaving Margaret an' Duncan on their ain
Great idea, Duncan-o

An' here we are another year
My, oh, my, how time has flown
Tae toast the bard once more oor aim
In rhyme, addresses, verse an' song
An' Rabbie looking on frae his lang hame
Is smiling tae himself an' saying
A wish tae damn, I could've came
It was a great idea, Duncan-o

Uncle Wullie

I made Wullie's acquaintance just the other day
He was resident at St. John's, courtesy o' the National Health
In the green bay
I was visiting an auld freen o' mine, wha lives just doon frae me
Also booked in at that brand new hospital for an MOT

There's a grand view o' the Pentlands
Through windows made by Weathershield
Stretching for miles and miles, snow on the hills an' fields
Well, a' was quiet and peaceful when suddenly there appeared
Relations an' freens o' Uncle Wullie, for a party they were geared

It seems it was the old man's birthday, they'd come tae wish him well
Wi' a birthday cake an' presents, he was very popular, I could tell
Well, their greetings were hilarious
You see, Uncle Wullie was quite deef
They each shouted, Happy Birthday, Uncle Wullie!
Auld Jimmy Young's expression clearly said, good grief!

For he was in the next bed, an' got roped into the melee
An' it was clear there was nae chance o' a blether
In peace an' quiet wi' me
There were nieces an' nephews a' gathered roon his bed
The old man, I could see, had recently lost a leg

They started tae open presents, this, Uncle Wullie, is for you
Stuck ear phones on the auld man's head
Gave him a wee transistor too
You can listen tae your favourite programme, they bawled into his lug
Na, na, Uncle Wullie, it disna' need a plug

Next came oot a trifle, A wee treat, it'll dae ye guid
Asked the nurse tae bring a knife, this the lassie promptly did
They a' sang Happy Birthday, Uncle Wullie
Then helped him cut the cake
Auld Jimmy sat there mesmerised, his een aff them he couldn'na take

But the highlight o' the party was something in a wee joug
They stuck a straw intae it and put it in his mooth
He sucked it wi' great relish, an' soon he'd sooked it a'
The transformation on Uncle Wullie soon was evident tae us a'

He was sat there smiling, surrounded by tender loving care
I felt really privileged that I happened tae be there
Time I left, I says tae Jimmy, tae Uncle Wullie I bade farewell
See an' bide sober noo, an' I hope you continue tae keep well

Nae fear o' that, says the auld man
It's no' every day I'm eighty-three
Just what the doctor ordered, says I tae Uncle Wullie
Aye, lassie, I agree

1989

For Son Michael's 40th Birthday

I couldn't let this day go by, wi' just the usual felicitations
For this birthday is quite different, son, nae need for hesitations
You've reached the age when life begins
Get oot and dae yer thing
Forget about they wee bit jobs, or whit the morning brings

Your school days are behind you, well and truly past
You'll hae many treasured memories, wi' Alistair Grant
    an' Alan Brash
Banging an' hammering bird boxes everywhere
You used tae get Lizzie Boyd right het up
Playing on her nice clean stair

Oh, the things you got up tae, dae ye mind Alan's braw wee car?
You and John Rankine decided you'd gie it a nice new coat of tar
Then the mystery of hoo Alistair Reid got a pellet through his wellies
Fired from the Reverend Wee Davie's air-gun
By you, you naughty fellow

When you got a bittie older, wi' golfing you became obsessed
Never mind, we've a' been right proud of ye
You're yin of Harburn's best
Just the other week at Kirk Michael's how-d'you-do
The name Mike Kirk stood oot a mile
Well done, son, good for you

Then you followed in yer faither's footsteps learned the trade frae
    A tae Z
Dae ye mind the time ye borrowed John's new shoes?
He didna half see red

Your faither had tae referee, he lowped oot o' his chair
An' ended the battle of the fancy shoes wi' oor Alice greetin' sair

Between working an' golfing, time flew swiftly by
You began a courtin' when this Polbeth lassie caught yer eye
Your mind was swiftly made up, marriage your next big step
Dae ye mind hoo you an' Gwen carried a double bed
Tae yer wee hoose in Gloag Place? You wouldna dae it noo, I bet

Along came Jackie and Michael, the usual ups and doons
Noo they too are grown up, the years fly past too soon
But there's still a lot tae dae and see
So just take the time an' dae it
Life could begin at forty, son
Take ma advice and make it

17 September 1989

Michael's Retirement

We've reached the age when once again
There's just two in the hoose
The nest flown, the young ones
Branched oot on their ain

You folk in the same age group as masel'
Will know what I mean only too well
An' noo that Michael has retired
My way of life has a' backfired

For the mair he sits in that big chair
The mair I think that life's no' fair
I've still the meals to make, the hoose tae clean
The washing, ironing etc, ken whit I mean?
While he sits back and gets waited on
I wonder where the devil I went wrong

I mean the modern husbands these days
Dry the dishes, hang oot the claes
They seem tae hae been licked into shape
But I'm afraid I've left it a wee bit late

If I go oot he'll ask, where are you gaen?
Oh, aye, oh weel, you'll no' be long
It's no' I don't enjoy his company
It's I'm no' used tae haen him in the hoose a' day

I had ma ain routine, was daen fine
The wee odd jaunt, when I felt inclined
Noo, I don't ken if I'm going or coming
Wha on earth wid be a woman?

I fling oot a few hints, gaen you make the tea
Well, wait a wee while, there's something guid on TV
Ye ken before ye git it, it'll be cheese on toast
For the next thing you hear is the smoke alarm gaen off

I say whit aboot a wee run, roon the Waterhoose on the bikes?
There's two in the garage yet, aye, that'll be right
Stephen Hendry's coming on, I'll need tae watch him
See wi' that box in the corner, ye jist canna win

But he's no' really had time tae settle doon
Whit wi' the war in the Gulf, earthquakes and monsoons

135

By the time he's watched the telly an' read a' the papers
I've been doon at the Co-op, the butcher an' bakers

But noo that the days are lengthening oot
An' things in the garden are beginning tae grow
Aye, Spring's roon the corner, ye ken whit they say
Live for the present, it'll soon slip away

The laddies built him a greenhouse
It was a surprise
An' wee John is gaen to lend him a fishing rod
An' gie him some of his flies

Oh, an' I got two British Rail cards
I've been using the heid
I'll just bide ma time, keep on trying
Until I succeed

I'll get him oot and aboot, if I hae tae dee in the attempt
I'm no' born under Taurus the bull for nothing, ye ken
He'll get used tae retirement sooner or later
An' as long as we've both got each other
Well! Wee things dinna matter

Jean Duncan was telling me, she's placed much the same
The difference being Hughie's hardly ever at hame
So it just goes to show, there's nae happy medium
Or as Michael would say, Women! You just canna please them

1990

Jimmy McQue's Retirement – The Ironmonger

It's sixty-seven years frae wee Jimmy McQue
Arrived on planet earth and made his debut
I can jist picture him, right chubby wee wean
His ma's pride and joy, destined for fame
He's lived in East Whitburn a' o' his life
A weel-kent face, where he met and mairrit Nettie, his wife
She came frae Seafield, no' far away
And they were mairrit in March, oh, happy day

Jimmy's a time-served joiner, that is his trade
The wee auld barraes, red inside, green outside, he's made
But one day he got tae thinkin, there must be an easier way
Tae eek oot a livin', no' be skint every week awaitin' yer pay
And since Watson's wee ironmongery shop wis due up for sale
Thought he'd try and buy it, it couldna fail
After a' he kent aboot things, like nuts, bolts and screws
He could advise folk and tell them the right kind to use
And he likes a guid blether wi' Jock, Bill and Tam
So put in an offer, it couldnae go wrang

So he went ahead and got it in nineteen-sixty-one
On the ladder o' success, Jimmy had his fit on the first rung
He taen ower the shop on April first, All Fool's Day
But he wis naebody's fool, oor wee Jimmy
Tae be his ain boss had aye been his aim
And he said one boss is enough, and I've got yin at hame

Oh, he did very well and soon was able to buy
Georgie Forrester's shop three years later, that is nae lie
He fair loved his shop and he thrived on the chaff

He had his ain brand o' humour, a swear and a laugh
For he loves conversation, it's one of his hobbies
Wi' folks frae a' walks o' life, priests, doctors or local bobbies

The other great love o' his life, apart frae Nettie, his wife
Is to go sequence dancing, aye, every week he goes twice
Of course, he's the head bummer, the president
He jist loves public speaking, gitting up and sayin' Ladies and Gents
He's nae stook, oor Jimmy, his home-grown tomatoes they say
    are simply divine
And last year he wis fair chuffed to see the first grape appear
    on his vine

Mary, Margaret and, of course, May, are sad he's retiring
But whit can they say?
At the thought of parting frae Jimmy, there's a tear in their ee
But, weel, that's how life goes, the years simply flee
As one door shuts, another opens, sometimes for the best
And lately I've noticed him leaning on the counter mair often
I think he's due a good rest

The 'Railway Inn' are goin tae miss him as weel
For he's aye slippin' in for a brandy and coffee, the de'il
Profits, I'd say, are bound tae be doon
When Jimmy makes his exit frae auld Cauther Toon

His one daughter, I hear, tae a dentist is wed
So apart frae his gold rings, watch etc
He's bound to hae a few gold teeth noo, I bet
And, of course, he's a proud grandpa, wi' a grandson he adores
And it's early days yet, he's hopin' for more

He loves holidays and travel, he's been a few places
He can still dae the tango, an' tie his ain laces

He also loves in the kitchen, makin' sausages and pies
But Nettie's warned him no' to eat ower many – at his age it widnae
    be wise

His prospecting days are aboot ower, I fear
But he must hae amassed quite a fortune, I'd say, ower the years
He should be able tae take Nettie on a round-the-world trip
Own a Rolls Royce like Pop Larkin, that would be perfick

So, here's tae a long, happy, healthy retirement and good luck to you
See you, Jimmy, you'll no' be forgot, whae could forget
    DEAR wee Jimmy McQue?

Oor John & Margaret's House Warming

We've a' gathered this Hogmanay in John and Margaret's
    new hoose
John, I think, like Jack an' the Beanstalk climbed up and grabbed
    the Golden Goose
He's had it in mind for a long time, I wid say
To build his ain hoose, he's done it an' he did it his way

It proves dreams do come true, but they can take a while
He can relax noo and sit back, look aroon wi' a smile
An' we're a' here tonight to launch the hoose, you could say
An' if you don't spill any drinks on Margaret's new carpet
We might get asked back some day

The drains gied them many a sleepless night
They were under the flairboards for a week, but try as they might
They just couldna find whit was causing the fault
But they finally did, it was their master bedroom pee pot

They must be really proud, an' they've a' lent a hand
An' Margaret, while inspecting the job, slipped doon through
   the joists and for a week couldna stand
She's some clerk o' works, never off that phone
An' she gets results, aye, they're some team, her an' oor John

But noo everything's aboot perfect, except for that ensuite loo
It's no' been replaced yet, so you can't hae a poo
But they've another two toilets so there's nae problem, you see
There's no need to queue, you can still a' hae a pee

They've a jacuzzi, they say, when shared can be quite fun
An' a power shower wi' a jet that reaches right up the bum
Patio doors lookin' on tae the famous Five Sisters bings
Sheep an' cattle grazin' doon by the drove loan an' birds on the wing

There's a full moon every night when you look oot the door
An' swans on a pond in the field in the distance
Whit man could ask for more?
There's peace and quiet, comfort an' style
An' a view frae their lounge window for miles an' miles

The Five Sisters

140

Aye, they must be right proud, and they've a' lent a hand
In building this fine hoose, it really is grand
May good health an' good fortune follow them to the end of life's road
May they live happily ever after, in their new abode

It appears as yet they've no' agreed on a name
But they're thinkin' on Kirkrig, well, good for them
If it's anything like Kiprig, that's where I was born
There's nothing left noo, but its memories live on
So here's tae the new Kirkrig, its laird and his wife
John Kirk, master joiner, first class, well done, here's tae a long life

31 December 1992

Hartwood Home Farm

It was called Hartwood Home Farm,
The auld farmhoose, noo Harrit Mains
It supplied the big hoose wi' all it required, milk, butter, eggs, tatties
    and game

It changed many, many times over the years
Employed numerous folk
In they days, ye haund-milked the kye
Tilled the land wi' horse, harness and yoke
Scattered the good seed tae left and tae right
Cut the corn wi' a binder, stoked and stacked it when it was ripe

Then along came the day for the big threshing mill
It went frae farm tae farm up and doon the hill
A busy time for the mistress, don't be misled
It wasnae only the threshing mill that had to be fed

The workers came to help and frae a' the farms aroon'
There could be mair than a dozen hungry men and women
At the big kitchen table sat doon
There was great camaraderie as they cut the sheaves and forked
Laughing and joking among theirsels
These doon-tae-earth country folk

The men roond their knees, strapped tight the auld nicky tams
For the wee field mice, in their hurry to escape, in gie weird places
    wid land
The wives frae the cottages wid then bring their bed tikes
Fill them wi' fresh chaff
Nothing was wasted, the straw used tae bed baith coo and calf

The harvest noo safely brought hame, the hard work
    mair or less done
A barn dance wid follow, always great fun
Harvest Thanksgiving was then held in the auld parish kirk
Adorned wi' sheaves of corn and barley, flowers
    and fruits of the earth
Nature glorified to the highest heaven above
They gave thanks to the Lord for all his goodness and love

Burns Night at The Hoose o' Collin – Two

I wonder whit oor bard wid say
If he'd tae pay a visit here today
He'd likely say, "Oh, help ma God
Whit has been going on in Hartwood Road?"

It used tae be a quiet wee place
Noo it's crammed wi' hooses, nae open space
Like mushrooms they hae quickly sprung
Wherever there's a bit o' grun'

They've multiplied quite rapidly
They're already half-roads up the brae
Even the auld schule, a housing complex has become
Hooses where the weans used tae play an' run
It's the same a' ower the countryside
Hooses, hooses far an' wide

Ye can hardly see a blade o' grass
A field o' buttercups are a thing o' the past
I hear tell they're negotiating the noo
Tae build on ma wee auld hoose
That's what they're fettling tae do

Aye, building hooses noo seems tae be the in thing
We'll be seeing them shortly on Addiewell Bing
Even the auld farm steadings are in demand
They're being made into dwelling hooses a' ower the land
Gie expensive yins at that
Nae happy hunting grounds noo for the auld farm cats

An' wha lives in these luxurious abodes?
Ye hardly see them, they've a' got jobs
For maist wives hae got their ain careers
Their grand hooses are jist for sleepin' in, it appears

They've every kind o' luxury
Made by man an' here tae stay
Once they get hame they sit for hours

An' watch a box that seems tae hae hypnotic powers
It keeps you informed of the latest news
An' gies other people's points o' views

You see some things ye'd rather no'
An' listen tae monie a tale o' woe
The only Neighbours noo ye're likely tae meet
Are the ones on the box frae Ramsay Street
Nae wonder whiles, that folk feel flat
They never find the time tae chat
Aye, ye miss a lot without a doot
When ye never take the time tae stop an' look

An' they auld folks hames that's a' sprung up
Where ye end yer days like some redundant tup
Na' I couldnae see masel' in there
They wid hae tae take the home helps intae care

Thank God I lived away back when
Oor valuables were oor coos and hens
A plate o' kale tae keep ye right
An' a blazing fire on a winter's night

I ken ma life was short and sweet
But oor values then were hard to beat
Oor health, oor freens, neighbours true
Times were hard but we got through

But it's nice tae ken I'm no' forgot
That ye still sing ma songs, an' poems quote
Even amidst the turmoils o' today
Ye still keep alive ma memory

Stewart Court Robert Burns Day

Weel, Rabbie, another year has passed
And we're here to toast ye, raise oor glass
Without fail, we dae it every year
We'll no' forget ye, never fear

We're still going strong at Stewart Court
A' gathered here, oor favourite folk
They look forward tae oor weekly bash
And the volunteers dae a job, first class

Bob and Archie, they take over the ropes
Recite or sing and tell some jokes
Martha, she excels hersel'
Sings the auld songs and sings them well

Wee Bella tae whiles gies us a song
And we a' join in the sing-along
Jean recites a poem she herself composed
And one from me helps keep them on their toes

We hae, of course, some weeks, a guest
Tae gie a talk or show us some slides frae East or West
The day-centre folk a' think it's great
And for next Tuesday they can hardly wait

Sometimes a resident does a turn
Mary Rankine recites, often something frae Burns
She's really great, ootshines us a'
She widnae be oot of place in the Usher Ha'

So, ye see, we're folk as likes much the same as yersel'
A wee dram, a song and some tales tae tell

145

That's whit we're here just for tae dae
Here's tae you, we salute your fond memory

As usual, I gie Rabbie an update on things worldwide
Well, there's still turmoil and wars happening an' woe betide
There's been floods and fires, an' earthquakes an' a'
An' when seen on the telly, it's no' very braw

There's a great problem the noo wi' folks taking drugs
Rape and murder, both weans and old folk being mugged
They're no' even exempt when at the school
They're playing games, an' it isn'a bools

The country's in bother, the government tae
MPs making headlines in the news every day
And they're the ones supposed tae show us hoo tae behave
An' they're a' breaking the rules, the situation is grave

Divorce, they say, is noo one in two
It's the puir weans that suffer, whit dae you do?
Marriage, it seems, there soon will no' be such a word
An' whae wants a man roon the hoose? Don't be absurd

Women sixty and over can noo hae a wean
They must be crazy, dae they ken whit they're daen?
They'll no' see them up or be there them to advise
It's some how-d'you-do, I don't think it's wise

Aye, they need us auld yins to show them just how
But I don't think they'd listen to us, somehow
So, Rabbie, you're better off where you are noo
We'll just have to hope for the best and keep smiling through

Stewart Court Day-Centre Burns Supper

It's nice to think in this day and age
Aboot this time of year it's still the rage
When the winter days are cauld and drear
We can meet the gither, oorsels tae cheer
Talk of things and times long gone
Keep a tryst wi' Burns in rhyme and song

Well-fed on haggis, neeps the lot
Or a plate of cockie-leekie, nice and hot
Some bannocks an' a guid bit cheese
Make a change frae mince and tatties an' green peas
But maist of a', ye canna beat, a dram or twa
When auld freens meet
Its magic power enables a'
To keep oot the wind, the sleet and snaw

Soon we're a' aglow, oor een alight
Relaxed and happy, just a wee bit tight
We hae a toast and then a song or two
A recitation tae remind us hoo
In days before the telly was invented
Folk on the whole were mair contented
They'd nae modern comforts we taen for granted
Like washing machines and electric blankets
Nae central heating, electric light or gas
Withoot which noo, I doubt if we wid last
Nae running water or double glazing
They'd tae heat the water, and wash theirsels in a tin basin

But content they were wi' their lot in life
A blazing fire and a comely wife

Guid neighbours when they needed them
Tae say come on in, come on ben
Hoo's yersel' and hoo's the weans?
And hoo's the auld yin's aches and pains?
I hear he's got hisel' back hame
Hoo's he managing on his ain?

Aye, times may change and fashions tae
But folk are still the same basically
An' if we're no' feelin' weel or fed up some day
A blether and a wee cup of tea are still guid therapy
We're still free tae choose oor freens and company
And that's what we've done at the day-centre today
So here's tae ye, Rabbie, you've no' been forgot
An' here's tae the next time frae your faithful fans in Stewart Court

Jenny & Wullie Anderson –
Ruby Wedding Anniversary

To the tune of 'Lily Marlene'

Jenny and Wullie went a courtin' while Britain was at war
Instead of beneath the lamplight, it was underneath the stars
Wullie used to lean his bike on the crossing gate
Wi' his carbine lamp, at a hut he'd wait
Then his sweetheart, Jenny, in his arms he'd take

As their courtship it developed, they thought they'd tie the knot
Wullie had surrendered, an engagement ring he bought
They were married at hame, in the room upstairs
A barn dance followed, for I was there
Then Jenny and her Wullie set off a happy pair

Their first night was spent at Douglas
In Rachel and Harry's upstairs room
I'm sure they will remember it, in history it went doon
After visiting the wee hoose oot the back
They'd a cup of tea and a friendly chat
Then off they went together, just like Jill and Jack

Jenny got her goonie on and settled doon in bed
Darling, put the light out and hurry up, she said
They'd just got in and cuddled doon
When the light came on, a' ower the room
My God, cried oot Jenny clutching tightly at her goon

Wullie jumped oot o' bed, and lookit a' in vain
Couldna find an answer, so turned the light back off again
They just got a' cosy under the claes
When the same thing happened, they banged up amazed
Wullie! Cried oot Jenny
This could go on a' night, she says

I'll hae tae get ma trousers on, says Wullie, and see whit can be wrang
They should hae stuck tae paraffin, he says, as doon the stairs
    he banged
But as he knocked quietly on the door
He heard a laugh – It's yous! He roared
Went back upstairs tae Jenny
Tae start again once more

They'd a honeymoon tae remember, that was forty years ago
Had two laddies, two lassies, and now five grandweans, as you know
They've been a' ower Scotland, wi' their dogs and hens
Their first hoose at Hermand, a but and ben
Their first move was tae Auchengray
Jim was just a toddler then

Then they went tae Broughton, tae a herding job this time
Wullie aye had the urge tae be a shepherd
A dream he always had in mind
The scenery was lovely and peaceful too
A great place for weans, among the sheep and coos
Content they were and happy
For another year or two

We joined them there ane summer, for a week we a' did bide
We a' went on manoeuvres, roon the Broughton countryside
Among the hills the weans did run
They had a great time, aye, it was fun
They a' loved their Auntie Jenny and her hame-made buns

Then they got the wanderlust and moved tae a place a mile or two
    away
I can never mind the name o' it, but it was a lonely place to stay
They did'na bide there very long
You know, like the words in that old song
They packed up their kit bags
And once again moved on

This time they moved tae Moffat, tae a cottage by the road
The Grey Mare's Tail was just along the way from their idyllic
    wee abode
They moved up and moved tae Cocksburnspath
It was by the sea, they didna need a bath
The next move was tae Sanquhar
By noo a guid few years had passed

Once again we spent a holiday among the rolling hills
There Jenny and Wullie both took pneumonia
Due tae cauld winter chills
'Twas there that Mary came on the scene
Jenny was forty but still young it seems

And so likewise was Wullie
Still in his eye yon gleam

The time came roon for marching, near Moniaive this time
'Twas there Mary learned the bagpipes, and she can play them fine
Jim got mairrit and Janet tae, they fledglings had grown up
    and flew away
Leaving Mary and William growing up quickly tae

Time had come for Wullie, nae mair route marches ower the hill
William taen ower the herding, his faither's boots he filled
Granny Kirk by noo was all alone
She stayed wi' them there off and on
Again we spent a summer
It was oor home frae home

Then they moved this time tae Thornhill
They were there a year or two
You could see Drumlanrig Castle in the distance, it was a lovely view
They'd a big farmhouse up on the hill
It was Mary this time who said, I will
Noo that just left William
A bachelor they thought until...

They spent a year in the Leadhills
The fishing there was great
That's where William hooked Shirley, who's soon tae be his mate
It was a lonely spot, nae hooses for miles
He could'na get oot for snow some whiles
To go and meet his Shirley
It fairly cramped his style

Well, noo they're up near Biggar, in a place called Flemington
The years have passed so quickly, forty years have come and gone
And Shirley and William are a' set to wed

A month from now they make their bed
As for Jenny and Wullie, a' their birds have fled

Their marching days will soon be over
Jenny's looking forward too
Just herself and Wullie, nae cats and dogs and coos
They're maybe no' the richest folks in town
But they're happy and content wi' their lot, I've found
Their door is ever open
Their welcome warm and sound

So, here's tae Jenny and her Wullie
The salt of the earth, their kind
They found the contentment some folk can never find
In their autumn years, by their ain fireside
May their memories of bygone years abide
Here's tae a well-earned retirement
Together, side by side

6 September 1986

Wullie and Jenny

For Rab & Betty Graham's Ruby Wedding

To the tune of 'Johnny Lad'

Rab met a a lass in Cauther Toon many years ago
He saw her at the dancin' an' thought, Hello, hello!
Whae's that lassie ower there wi' the braw dark curly hair?
I could dance the buckles aff her shin, an' aff he shot across the flair

His technique, weel if ye ken Rab, left much tae be desired
Being a Sergeant in the army, a few choice words at her he fired
Let's see if your feet can keep in step wi' mine
I'll dance the buckles aff yer shin
An' they did just that, an' got on fine

He manoeuvred her right brawly, tae the music they kept time
Rab wis aye first across the flair, he couldna' get Betty oot his mind
So he played that age-auld game
Saying, Can I walk you oot tae Loganlea?
An' marched back in again

Noo, Betty, she wisna' very auld, an' still wis in the WRENS
When the Dundas's got word o' their romance
They said, Haud on a meenit, hen
He's a guid bitty aulder, the rough and ready type
Are ye shair he's the man for you?
Dae ye think ye're daen' right?

They were mairrit in nineteen-fifty-one in the month o' February
They settled doon in Back Street, where the legion is today
They'd twa lassies an' twa lads
An' their life wis no' that bad
Rab danced the buckles aff her shin
Every chance he had

Rab he wis a postman, weel kent up The Whang
He ran messages for the shepherd folk, an' gied the farms a bit haun
A leader in the Boys Brigade
The big drummer in the Pipe Band
He'd nae time tae dance the buckles aff her shin
He wis never in, be damned

He was also in the Glebe Singers, and once sang on radio
He kept at yin time collie dugs, Betty often thought, Oh, No!
I never ken whit tae expect
Whit will he get up tae next?
It's years frae he danced the buckles aff ma shin
I hardly see the get

They spent maist o' their mairrit life in Polbeth, changed hooses
    ain or twice
Betty also was in a ladies choir
Rab wasna the only ane wi' a singing voice
For Betty's auld dad saved his pocket money up hard
To pay for singing lessons for his wee Betty
Wisna he a clever lad

Noo, Betty wisna just a pretty face, she'd monie talents, so had she
A guid housewife an' mother
Wi' nursing capabilities
The family are a' prood o' her, an' Rab, of course, as weel
She brought oot the best in him
He'll tell ye that hisel'

When he retired, she took a warden post, doon at Mansefield Court
Rab worked hand in hand wi' her
A great help tae they auld folk
Aye, so we see, whit will be will be
They also went a trip tae Canada
An' had a lovely holiday

They're getting set noo for Betty tae retire an' hae a well-earned rest
They got a caravan in Comrie, they ca' it their love nest
For he's still the same auld Rab
Wi' plenty patter an' gab
He's goin' tae dance the buckles aff her shin
Even though he's a grandad

There's twa names I'd like tae mention, that's their auld pals
     Nan and Wullie Steel
They emigrated tae Australia an' I hear they're daein weel
They're missed here the night
So I think it only right
That absent freens be remembered
Even though they're oot o' sight

So here's tae Rab and Betty, forty years later on
They've survived life's ups and doons an' still they're going strong
They've up tae noo, got seven grandweans
An' as Godfather he now reigns
They're goin' tae dance the buckles aff their shin
An' enjoy this evening's fun an' games

February 1991

Uncle Wullie's 60th Birthday

Wullie was born in nineteen-thirty-two
A change o' life wean, he caused a bit of a do
His mammy had thought she'd finished breastfeedin' for good
An' the auld pram was noo a bogie, lying somewhere between
Crosswood Burn an' Crosswood

But, as they say, what will be will be
She was back once again taking a wee boy for a wee
He was blessed wi' twa sisters an' a big brother tae
To run after him an' watch oot he didna stray

For toys, unlike the weans of today, he didna hae much
But when he got bigger, he kept rabbits roon the back in a hutch
I think that's where he learnt aboot the birds and the bees
It came in handy when his ma' taen in two evacuees
Girls they were, and stayed aboot two years until the war ended
I'll no' say ony mair, the less said soonest mended

He grew up an' left school, started work wi' his brother
Left and did his National Service, wi' some advice frae his mother
Whatever ye dae, don't bring back a wife
I'm no' that fond o' they English, I ken whit they're like

However, that's just whit oor Wullie did
For withoot his wee Myra, he said he just couldna live
Along came the weans – a boy and a girl
The years just rolled by in a whirl

Then along wi' his big brother they branched oot on their ain
Tae hae their ain business, that was their aim
They built their ain hooses, just like oor John
They prospered an' did very well, the years rolled along
Then they bought an old pub, an investment, they said
It proved to be just that, a nest egg for their auld age

An', of course, he's a proud grandpa, has been for a while
He plays the role o' Godfather, and Myra sits back and smiles
When the wee yins go away hame, he's depressed for a week
He sits in the dumps wi' a hauf an' has a bit greet

He's still hale an' hearty except for his gout
It gies him the gyp as he hirples about
Well, noo his big brother's retired an' Wullie's well on the way
He's maturing quite nicely, he's sixty today

So many happy returns, I ken it's a wee bitty late
I just took this chance as we a' congregate
To bring in the New Year, an' many more may you see
Cheers, a' the best Wullie
Frae your big brother an' me

31 December 1992

Burns Night at The Hoose o' Collin – Three

Weel, John, as you know
Has lived some years in Hartwood Row
An' it seems he's got us a' sized up
Whit we dae, an' where we work
Kens a' there is tae ken
Aboot a' us wee chookie hens
An' watches daily as we scrape an' scart
The big cock-a-doodle-do, in his favourite patch

Noo, it seems I'm tae reply to Mr John Gilmour
Who happens tae live across the road frae me, practically next door
I see he's planning tae move hoose
Tae pastures new, flies the Gilmour goose
Tae spread his wings and preen his feathers
An' get another view o' Cauther lassies all together

Weel, they do say a change is as good as a rest
Before very long we'll see him at his best
Viewing the world through rose-coloured glasses
Like Rabbie, oor John'll be surveying the lassies

But mind, they've a' progressed frae Rabbie's day
They're mair independent, go oot tae work noo, and, of course
    hae their say
Gone are the days when women slaved frae morning till night
Keepin' the hooses, keeping the peace, seein' a' body was a' right
I'm no' saying men didna work hard and handed ower the pay
But there their problems ended, that was the auld way

Noo these days are gone, for better or for worse
Men darena go oot, get drunk, an' come hame, shout, swear or curse
Noo the women winnae tolerate chauvinistic men
Equality is whit it's a' aboot noo, we can keep up wi' them

We've women doctors, lawyers an' ministers, nothing for them's
    taboo
Nae mair dae we gan out shaw turnips, feed hens, milk the coo
Aye, they've no' hauf made progress, we also hae the right
To say, No, no, dear, I'm sorry I don't feel like it
Nae hanky-panky the night

This is the night for ma aerobics, you ken I'll come back dead beat
Let me see if I can fit you in, wid Wednesday dae? Next week!
But see if I get a cancellation, remind me later on
Oh, an' wid you put the weans tae bed?
I might be late in getting home

Then they've also got that daily pill, birth control, it's caud
Eight grandweans is enough for any granny, when they come
    visitin', thank the Lord!

It wasna aroon in ma day, but then neither was sliced breed
We'd tae cross oor fingers, count the calendar, and try no' tae lose
the heid

But sayin' that, we somehoo managed tae survive an' live tae tell
the tale
It wid hae been a strange unexciting world, if we'd a' been born
female
So, you see, you're still needed, lads, and you need us tae trigger
That inbuilt mechanism, an' it's a gie auld horse, that disna nicker
So, all hail tae the laddies, without them, whatever wid we dae?
You help keep us on an even keel an' we widna want it any other way

The Bus Trip to Ireland

We went on a bus trip to Ireland to view old Erin's green isle
The scenery it was stupendous – green fields and hills for miles
and miles
The weather it was just perfect the soft winds like thistle down
And the water you washed and made tea with was a lovely dark
shade of brown

White cottages dotted all over, blending the old with the new
Wee houses surrounded by roses and named
Lark Mist, Green Peace and Sea View
It was all so relaxing, making new friends on the way
Laughing and joking together, dead tired at the end of each day

We saw where the Spanish Armada limped into a sheltering bay
You can still see the Spanish connection, young folk with dark
Latin looks to this day

We saw a memorial statue, a small boy, hands outstretched to a door
Starving in rags, a reminder o' that great famine of yore

The dry stone dykes so artistic, stretching over hill and over vale
A masterpiece there on the landscape, built to withstand
    the Atlantic gales
We passed Tully's off-licence, Meg McGuire's Bar and Rafferty's Nest
Sampled the famous Guinness, had a jar of Jamieson's best

We went on to beautiful Galway, had a guided tour enjoyed by all
The cathedral was quite majestic, the stonework left us all enthralled
Yes, it was well worth the visit on that beautiful August day
We can all say we've been to Galway and saw the sun as it shone
    on the bay

We searched for a four-leafed clover, didn't find one, needless to say
It was a ploy to catch everyone bending, high on a hill top that day
We saw horses and ponies, donkeys, cows, sheep, goats and hens
Went up hills and down hills, round corners
That made the hairs on your neck stand on end

We saw the great river Shannon as it meandered to the sea
Stopped at Bunratty Castle, where we enjoyed a nice cup of tea
Saw the Burren's flora and fauna crammed along the hedgerows
Cliffs and rocks along the coastlines, fields where the wild flowers
    grow

Yes, Ireland was well worth the visit
Something to look back on when you go home
Memories to last us a lifetime, more precious than silver or gold
Friends we'll sometimes remember, as we sit back and smile
We'll say, wasn't that a grand week we spent in the Emerald Isle?

Harburn Hall

This is a story, I think might interest you all
You could say it's an autobiography of Harburn Hall
Now, just imagine if it had the power of speech, even for a day
The story it could tell would go like this, I'd say:

Before coming here, I was on active service, that was many years ago
Very young and smart I was then, and many grand lads I used to know
Oh, I did my bit in the 1914–18 for my country and my King
I've seen it all, you can't tell me, war's a dreadful thing

Eventually I was demobbed and went to this outlandish place
It was awful settling down to civvie life, I missed the other huts
    around the base
Don't get me wrong, the folk roon here treated me wi' kindly care
Saw to my every need and did their best to keep me in good repair

At first, the trains on that railway gave me many a fright
Especially when they thundered past in the middle of the night
When I complained, they said I should be honoured
Many Kings and Queens have passed this way
On their journeys up and doon frae London, yes, I've seen the day

Oh, I soon got used to it, but at first I thought I'd never
And even when they go fleeting past, I can feel ma timbers shiver
I settled doon tae their ways o' life, got tae ken them all frae
    the shepherd tae the laird
Monie's the tale that I could tell, but don't worry, I've been well dared

There's been many grand functions held in here, folk came frae
    near and far
By shanks' pony and bicycle, long before they had motorcars

They met auld freens, made new yins, some even found a wife
Aye, to a guid few folks sitting oot there the noo
Here marks the first milestone on the road to mairrit life

Yes, I even played cupid in my day, and fired my little darts
Underneath this dress of mine, it managed to pierce my heart
I've seen ceilidhs and whist drives, and dances by the score
They've hooched and danced tae the wee sma' oors upon
    my wooden floor
I've listened tae the bagpipes at Burns' Suppers until I felt
    my rafters birl
I ken weel hoo Tam O' Shanter felt when his heid was in a whirl

At times ootside the wind would howl, an' there'd be lots o' snaw
But it didnae seem tae worry them, they had nae cares at a'
They were all there tae enjoy thersels, they would worry about
    that later
They aye got back their separate ways, well fortified wi' a guid
    drop o' the craitur

I thought I'd never see another war, but unfortunately I did
Oh, will mankind never learn, to live and, as they say, let live?
Once again, we a' got prepared for action, this time Dad's Army
    was all the go
But there was the ARP and the Home Guard, as some of you will know

It was a long time ago and ma memories are faded
And maybe it's a good job we never were invaded
After the war, things got slowly back to normal, the country got
    back on its feet
Folk were beginning to get gaen' again, like wakening oot a sleep

I will say I did enjoy the weddings here, real family affairs
Everyone in their Sunday best, to launch the happy pair
I've watched their progress all through life, saw their families grow

Until they too did the self same thing, and onwards through life
     they'd go
I've gied my services as the Lord's hoose on a Sunday
And emerged reassured and strengthened to face another Monday

A while ago, I must admit, I began to feel ma age
I let masel' get run doon, things went all wrong, I had reached
     the menopausal stage
And to crown it a', a few years back I thought ma end had come
A great big tree fell on top of me, in the region of ma bum

They managed to patch me up again, replace that vital part
But it was a while 'ere I got over the shock, yes, it gave me quite a start
Then the damp crept in and made my life a misery
That old stove had me near choked
I was falling into depression and beginning to gie up hope

But I didnae bargain on a' ma freens, and how they rallied roon
They up and got a fund started, and do you know, very soon
Plans for a much needed operation were quickly underway
For a while I was in an awfy state, but improved slowly every day

Some kind lassies applied all the new make-up, while the laddies
     undertook
Their best to get me on ma pins again, withoot disturbing a' ma roots
And gradually, wi' all the tender loving care, I came into ma ain
I feel I've got ma second wind, I've been reborn again

The bairns at the nursery school don't seem to annoy me any mair
I fair enjoy seeing the young ones at the Youth Club letting doon
     their hair
And the Women's Rural fairly grew in numbers, right clever bunch
     we've got
The cups for competitions, you can bet, they nearly always lift the lot

Their latest ploy – the drama group – monie's a laugh I get
At all the budding actresses and their antics on the set
Yes, when you're happy, I'm happy, that's just hoo life goes
I feel for you in times of stress when winds do harshly blow

So, you see, I'm almost human, though no' made of flesh and blood
I too hae had ma ups and doons, but you just mark ma words
Here I am, and for a long time yet, here I hope to stay
They say old soldiers never die, they only fade away

Oh, I've seen a lot of changes, and there'll be a lot to come
I'll sit quietly in ma corner, be a looker-on, as in the past I've done
Thank you for being such good listeners, oh, and by the way
The best of luck tae your drama group, I really like their play

PostScript – Seventieth anniversary of Harburn Hall

Just to keep you up to date, I've another episode for you
They tell me it's seventy years – would you believe? Aye, seventy
    years, it's true
Since I came to live among you, volunteered to do my bit
The Community Council are wondering, if I am still up to it

I've had to sit another medical, they say at my age, just routine
A lot of red tape and regulations, you all know what I mean
They tell me I need some new equipment, a fire door is a must
You would'na like to see me burned right to the ground, reduced to
    a pile of dust

No, I'm still needed roon here, I've a few good years left yet
And tonight we hope to raise some pounds just to keep me out of debt
You see, there's a query about my floorboards, they think I might
    have a wee prolapse
They've had to do an exploratory, I'm awaiting the result of that

164

To fix these things you need money, a word that's often mentioned
And, well, you see, noo, I'm only on the pension
And winter takes its toll on me, I mind once in sixty-five
I needed a major operation, to help me keep alive
As usual, funds were at their lowest, there was no way I could pay
That's when Michael said he'd give his services free of charge
For the Hall held fond memories

Yes, for him and many others too numerous to name
When they were all young and gay and they played the mating game
Well, anyway, Wullie Brash did assist him, and everything went
    as planned
I find there's always somebody keen to lend a helping hand

165

Look how, once again, folk have rallied roon, donating prizes
    for tonight's draw
I'm fair at a loss for words, I can only thank you a'

Do you like my new chairs and tables? They transform the place
A birthday present from the Women's Rural, they help me out
    in so many ways
They laid on this birthday party, and Jean Duncan's made the cake
And Mrs Leslie's going to help me blow the candles out
We go back a long way, me and Kay

It's great to see old friends and neighbours and so many new faces too
I hope you all enjoy my birthday party
Once again I say a big thank you

9 October 1993

Harburn Hall – Phase Two

This is another update, on the saga of Harburn Hall
It seems that in this day and age
I don't come up to environmental standards at all
There's nae hot running water, only one sink – it's taboo
Makes you wonder hoo on earth for seventy-six years we managed
    perfectly somehoo

You're no' allowed tae cook meals in the kitchen
It's been declared a danger zone
Where for years we've enjoyed a plate o' stovies
Or made soup wi' a great big marrow bone
Noo, a' these new germs and viruses
Waiting tae pounce where an' when they can
Causing great discomfort, you're never aff the lavvy pan

166

Then there's no' enough toilets, weel, I can mind back when
There was one for all the women and nane at a' for the men
They just went ootside for a smoke, chose either East or West
It didna' present a problem,
They aye reckoned it was guid for the grass

While they were ootside maist men sneaked a nip
As alcohol was not allowed on the premises
But it was always there, in a wee flask on the hip

Hence the reason they've got this project underway
Great plans they've got in store for me
A' the improvements they're gonna make
Just you wait and see

I'll be keeping an eye on a' the comings and goings as I usually do,
    I've had plenty practice ower the years
I'm very observant an' can be the soul of discretion, never fear
Ma appearance tae the passerby will thankfully remain the same
I rather like frae that angle, the wee photo John Wilkinson taen
For years I've led a sheltered life next to the railway track
Noo when I make the headlines, I feel quite famous
Weel and truly on the map

Ma military upbringing has gien me the courage tae keep on
    going on
When I found mysel' in a tight corner, I aye kent I was no' alone
An' here I am once again, I'm sending oot an S.O.S
I need assistance urgently
I need the right equipment tae get me oot this mess

This will probably be ma last campaign, ma life depends on you
Get reinforcements underway, an' the battle's half won
Aye, that's true

Once these alterations are accomplished, there's nae saying where
   I'm heading
You'll need tae book me in advance for your big society wedding

Ma imagination's running riot, for ma official opening
Why no' ask the Queen?
If she can come an' dae the honours at Bentyhead, well, one must
   hae a dream
Which brings me back tae this project, this mammoth campaign
Wi' a bit o' help frae the auld brigade, I'll be back in action again
Ready willing and able tae serve the community
Who knows, for services tae Harburn
I might yet receive the O.B.E.

23 January 2002

Harburn Hall – Completion

Well, here we are, it's the seventh o' May
A' the hard work an' fundraising in the past
Hip, hip, hooray!
The auld Hall, once again, has got a new lease of life
It's onwards and upwards, everyone happy and smiling tonight

It's no' that long ago it seemed to be doomed
Declared unhygienic, substandard, it might need knockin' doon
They couldna hae that, it wid be like losing ane o' their ain
It had been a landmark roon here for years, they'd need tae a'
   think again

So they got the gither tae see whit they could dae
If they could just raise the cash, there might be a way

Mind, it's eighty years auld, its no' had a bad life
It's had a few setbacks, ta'en a few blows ance or twice

But it's aye had the ability, wi' a help frae auld freens
Tae get up an' get goin' again, ken whit I mean
So it's up once again, tae dae whit ever it takes
Tae keep it alive, keep marching on, for auld times' sake

The fund raising began in earnest right away
First they'd apply for a grant frae the National Lottery
Then they appealed tae the council, see if they'd ony siller tae spare
If desperate, they could haud up the bank
There's plenty doon there

Oh, there's numerous ways that sprang tae mind
Haud tae ransom some rich millionaire, wi' pockets weel-lined
They might haud a few concerts
Ceilidhs and things
But the kind o' money they're needing
Nae enough wid that bring

But if a' else fails, they could get doon on their knees
Ask the good Lord above tae answer their pleas
I believe they did that an' he listened tae whit they had tae say
For them that seek, there's always a way

That's whit they did, they searched here and there, pulled a few strings
An' believe it or no', the monies started rolling in
Then on Sundays, the local workforce arrived in their auld
    workin' claes
Stripped the place completely bare
Thus completing the first phase

They found lots of memorabilia frae the fifties
Songsheets, newspapers, scripts, skittles an' carpet bools
An empty Craven A pack, stamped wi' the black cat
Frae the days when to smoke was considered cool
A moose's nest, built tae last, weel hidden frae view
By the size o' it, each year they'd added an extension new

String, paper, plastic, wool, rags an' fluff
They sure knew where tae build it, keep it cosy, nice an' snug
Well-insulated, refurbished before cauld winter blast
They'd coorie in an' settle doon, till warmer winds arrived at last

Once the dust had settled doon, they cleared away the awful mess
Next on the scene, the tradesmen, tae dae whit they dae the best
The new toilets, you'll find, are deluxe, unisex
Plenty for a', four in a row, like clookin' hens sat in a nest

A brand new stage also, that can be quickly moved elsewhere
The very latest up-tae-date kitchen
Plenty room, you could waltz across the flair

Of course, a' the little extras, tae make it all complete
You can sit an' enjoy your meal noo
An' no' be feart tae eat

Whit a transformation, so much bigger noo inside
Like an auld photograph that's been enlarged, fair swollen up
    wi' pride
New weather cladding on the outside
Up-tae-date windaes – double-glazed
A once-defunct surplus army hut
Another piece of memorabilia fae a byegone age

I've heard a whisper the best is yet to come
Tarmac! Look out weeds an' nettles you've no' much longer noo
    tae run
Courtesy o' the Cooncil plus a lamp-post outside tae light the way
They've thought o' everything
There's no' much more tae say

It's still kept its appearance though, an' tae them who chance
    tae wander by
They might be forgiven in thinking
It's Harburn Headquarters – a training camp for the S.W.R.I.

Noo, I think the last word must be for the Hall
It wid like tae convey its thanks tae you all
In future it hopes tae haud many events
Ceilidhs, concerts, birthdays, weddings, whatever
All can be managed at a nominal rent

Meanwhile it's going tae enjoy lookin' back at those happy auld days
Wi' a' its auld freens, many who've gone their different ways
An' of course, here's tae the future, an' many more moons
There it is, time tae ca' a halt, an' for me tae step doon

7 May 2004

Coortin! 1995 Style

In this day and age, in every paper there's a page
Where you can place an ad for someone very special
You can contact a mate at a reasonable rate
It's simple, safe and confidential

If you're lonely or sad, a lassie or a lad
A one-parent dad or mum
Who would like to meet someone discreet
Phone now, no sooner said than done

You might place an ad saying, I've got my ain pad
A company car, I'm male aged thirty-three
I'm looking for a girl, I could take out for a birl
And who, in time, might come tae love me

Or, my name is Ann, phone me if you can
I'm not bad looking, single, thirty-four
I've been engaged twice, not met the love of my life
So phone me if you want to ken more

Or how about Bill? I'm hoping to fill
An aching, vacant place in my heart
I like travelling and sailing, looking for someone who's caring
And can bake a nice apple tart

Although I'm seventy-four, my athletic days are o'er
But I can still make a guid cup of tea
So if you've time to spare and can still climb the stair
Ring me on 871 203

Or what about – I'm sixty, mature, love gardening, I'm sure
There must be someone, somewhere for me
We'd aim at friendship for a while and I'd add with a smile
Who knows? We can but wait and see

Then again, I'm a one-parent dad, with a lass and a lad
So you see my social life is quite nil
I'm hoping to find someone caring and kind
Someone special around thirty, my life to fill

I'm five-feet-five, dark hair and blue eyes
Please phone me, I'm fed up on my own
I'm forty, female, unattached and still not met my match
I need someone to make my house a home

Then again, I'm awfully shy, that is, of course, why
I'm appealing for the girl of my dreams
Who would love me as I am, and wouldn't give a damn
If I only could make tea and toast and beans

Or, I'm sixty-plus, got my pass for the bus
But no' o'er the hill yet, I'd say
Just give me a ring and dae yer ain thing
Like Sinatra, we could dae it my way

I've a wee ferm o' my ain and twa laddies still at hame
Who don't appear to be looking for a wife
So on behalf of the pair, is there twa lassies oot there?
I'd like tae see them mairrit and so would ma wife

I'm female, twenty-two, have a room with a view
And no-one to share it, as yet
Won't some hunky male, serenade under my balcony rail?
Be my Romeo, I'll be your Juliet

Rag Rugs

I see linoleum's making a comeback
And rag rugs are back in fashion too
Why don't you all try making one?
Recycle your old wardrobe, an excuse, come Spring
    for something new
It helps pass the time, these long dark nights, and it's also
    great therapy
It keeps you busy, chases boredom, especially on dull wet days

Christmas and New Year over, that's the time to make a start
Whoever is the most artistic, draws a pattern on a hessian sack
Unpick the old clothes, cut them into strips
Red and yellow, brown, black, green and blue
Old jerseys, scarves, socks, skirts and cardies
Even your old coat will do

In fact, you can get quite nostalgic
Over certain items now and then
A woollen dress you got one Christmas for a party
Remembering when last you wore it, where and when
A dressing gown, no longer needed
Well worn and sadly out of date
Before you installed central heating
To see it all worked in, I cannae wait

There's two of Mikey's old golfing jerseys
Pringle, no less, nice and bright
The very thing for my rag rug
And here's a pair of my old woollen tights
They seem to have shrunk a bit in the washing
Naw! Who am I trying to kid?
I've not been watching the calories, I think it's now high time I did

What's this? Some of Sarah and Hayley's cast-offs
It's a sin to cut them up
See these two 17-year-olds! Oh, I'd better just shut up
Every rag tells a story, as you work those old clothes in
But at least they'll have a longer life span this way
Better than ending up in some wheelie bin

As you start your masterpiece, work it bit by bit each day
The housework, ironing, get neglected
You become addicted, I would say
It's February and nearly finished, the nights are longer now and soon
Thoughts of spring cleaning come into mind
You picture the new rug in the living room

There you are, the winter's nearly over
With satisfaction you're aglow
Some of you achieve the same effect
By painting, quilting or just to knit and sew
Why don't you try the rag rug making?
Something you can just sit back and admire
It costs next to nothing, just time and effort, sitting cosy by the fire

1996

Bella & Michael's Golden Wedding in Harburn Hall

Our Golden anniversary, can it really be
Fifty years ago since I took you, you took me?
For richer for poorer, for better or for worse
In sickness and in health, here we are, the pair of us

Back to where we started, oh, so long ago
Would we have done things differently? The answer is no

In the year forty-seven, marriage was certainly in fashion
Even oor present Queen and her consort were caught in the web
    of desire, passion

And how it all came aboot, I'm sure you're a' dying to hear
You can turn your hearing aid up or down, as you wish, my dear

It starts with a once upon a time story, a long time ago
About a young upstairs-downstairs maid, and how she first got
    to know
A young country joiner, employed by the local pit baron
Who was sent to repairs at the family estate and adjoining home farm

We had afternoon tea in the kitchens with the mistress's consent
He thanked me most kindly, then off he went
I remember it clearly, a real nice laddie he seemed
But as for meeting up with him again at some point in life
    I never dreamed

But I call it providence, destiny, or just plain fate
Friends persuaded me to go to a dance in this very hall at a much
    later date
It was the first time I had been, and what do you know?
Standing there in a corner, were three handsome lads in a row

Cousins, they turned out to be, not unlike one another
Two with lovely dark wavy hair, they could have been brothers
But the one in the middle, at a glance I could see
Was the young joiner laddie and he recognised me
Well, there you are, be it providence or chance
The start, shall we say, of the adventures and exploits of romance

There were nae phones in those days, or cars in which to snog
Just your three-speed Raleigh bike tae get you up and doon
    The Whang, through wind, hail, rain and fog

And see that winter of forty-seven! Snowdrifts for miles aroon'
You could'nae walk, far less cycle, for weeks we were marooned

So Michael says, We'll get married, I'm nae trekking these roads
    another winter again
I'm fed up getting soaking wet day after day in sleet, snow, hail
    and rain
No need in those days to place an ad in the local papers
It was the usual conclusion maist folk arrived at, after a period
    of high jinx and capers

So a wedding was arranged, we picked our best maid an' best man
Sadly no longer with us, but we can't forget Tam
We were married on a Friday, the afternoon – p.m.
That's when maist folk got married, after their working week came
    to an end

In these days everything was in short supply
Coupons, units, dockets for bread, food and meat, furniture
    and clothes forby
How to cater for a wedding was a big headache
Thank goodness Michael's folk kept a coo and some hens – at least
    we had a cake

Friends and neighbours rallied roon, they borrowed this and that
The barter system came in handy – fruit and veg for some sugar
    butter or some marg
I don't know how they managed it, but they produced a lovely spread
A miracle, just like the story of the loaves and fishes, the multitude
    was fed

In the process Ma Kirk's table cover went missing, some cups
    and saucers tae
Someone must hae needed them badly but I had tae replace them
    at a later day

Bella

Michael

Worldly goods we had nane, so there was nae problem there
We were grateful for the bits and pieces given to us by folk who
    had use for them nae mair

There were no expensive presents, there was nane to be got
And the honeymoon was a long weekend in Costa Del Milnathort!

Our first but an' ben had paraffin lamps and an outside loo
A tap wi' cold running water, but like many another we all made do
You went to bed early on cold winter nights
And that year the birth-rate rose all o'er the country, it's true
    aye, that's right

The family began to arrive at regular intervals without fail
I was kept busy running out to the loo wi' a galvanised pail
That was in the days of free orange juice and cod liver oil
The old scrubbing board and the smell of terry-towelling nappies
    on the boil

And no washing them or hanging them out on a Sunday
    and offending those good Christian folk
You had to wait till a Monday before hanging out your clothes rope

Of course, there was just one wage coming in
So Michael did homers at night and weekends, that he did
    good for him
He had always hoped one day to work for himsel'
He took the big step forward in fifty-six, he thought it out well
Wullie would keep on his job, and they would share the one
    wage packet
Yes, we were hard up at times, but we just kept at it

Things gradually improved and by now we had four weans growing
    up fast
He set to and built us a house and after two years hard work
    we moved in at last

As time moved on, Michael and John started work with Kirk Brothers
And in the years that followed, their sons joined them to work
    with the others

We've both retired now, have been for some years
Michael still loves to work with the tools and keep busy
    although we've both dropped down to low gear

We've a family to be proud o', things have worked out very well
Nine grandchildren, one great grandson – that speaks for itsel'
For a marriage, you must give and take
There's a force out there somewhere, dictates who you choose
    for a mate

If you want it to last, a big lot is up to yoursel'
There's none of us perfect, no', not even masel'
Well, folks, there it is, only one thing more to say
I'm thankful we've both got each other's love and support
    this late on in the day

19 September 1997

Royal Summons

We were lucky enough to receive an invite by Royal Command
To the Garden Party at Holyrood in June, I've never been at any-
    thing before quite so grand
Michael says, Bella, you'll need to go and buy yourself a nice new frock
Indeed I will not, I replied, the Queen's never seen me
In the last ane I bought

I've no' had it on for quite a long time
I think it still fits me, aye, it'll dae fine

181

Then I've ma navy blue shoes, they'll dae as weel
I'll take them tae the cobblers, they're just needing heeled
I'll see if Jean's got a hat – a nice dark blue
And I'll gie yer guid suit a press – that'll dae you

We arrived at the gates, there were over eight thousand folks
Not a soul that we kent, except some of the Government blokes
We saw the Queen and Prince Philip, they too being fifty years wed
I thought, they're no' unlike oorsels, and they've had their ups
    and doons tae
So it's been said
She's a typical Taurus, just like masel'
I think her an' I could hae got on very well

So here's to Her Majesty, good health, long may she reign
And if it's no' asking too much, Lord, could you grant us the same?
I don't want to be greedy, we've both passed our three score and ten
We've been lucky so far, but, well, you never know when
We're quite prepared to take life as it comes
But we'd still like to be around in the Millennium

The Life of Burns

Twa hundred years have passed and mair since Robert Burns
    was born
Amidst a gale, no' unlike the one we had the ither morn
His parents were of farming stock, though small and very poor
Were hardworking, honest, country folk
His faither, perhaps, though dour
Was a man of great intelligence, far above his station
At least that's the impression I got frae watching
Burns's Life on television

Robert was the eldest of a family of seven
He and his brothers had to help in the daily toil to earn a living
And from an early age, he was often plagued
By depression and bad heads
Nae doubt the cause was mainly worry, overwork
And mostly being underfed

And as time passed, he became aware there were other things in life
Things that made life worthwhile
Where he could forget the strain and strife
And as he toiled at the plough, his thoughts would drift elsewhere
To some sweet, bonnie, sonsie lass and the colour o' her hair

All through his life they inspired him and played a major part
At times he displeased his faither sair
And must have broke his mither's heart

Aye, for maybe Rabbie loved the lassies, but his love was aye sincere
Whether it was Peggy, Nell or Bess, every one to him was dear

But there is one, I think, who stands apart in Robert Burns's life
It's his patient, loving Bonnie Jean, his gentle-hearted wife
She accepted all his weaknesses that we're all subject to at whiles
To her, he was her handsome Rab on whom dame fortune smiled

His poems and songs still famous yet, even after a' they years
Songs that reach your very heart, and fill your een with tears
They say the good that men do live after them, so as long as the
    rivers run
His name will be remembered, Immortal Rabbie Burns

Sandra & Eric Dobson's Silver Wedding

Through the years they've progressed, worked really hard
Extended the house, cut down the trees, cleared the old station yard
They took their time, didn't rush things as they went on life's way
You know the old saying, Rome wasn't built in a day

I think they're still working on the house, their home sweet home
It's been as big a project as the Millennium Dome
They aim to finish it in plenty of time
To usher in the year 2000, that's the deadline

Eric started his own business, it had always been his dream
Sandra still works in the bank, she's in this and that, and she cooks
    and cleans

184

She's a staunch member of the S.W.R.I. and everything connected
    to Harburn Hall
When the drama and pantomime season's in full swing Eric hardly
    sees her at all

But he's into clay pigeon shooting among other things
And once a month he meets his mates in the club house
Time has flown by so swiftly like a bird on the wing

The boys are following in Dad's footsteps, learning his trade
I'm sure given time they'll both make the grade
They've achieved a lot over the years, you can tell
As Brucie says, Didn't they do well?

They've settled down in Harburn, made many good friends
Always there when and where needed a helping hand ready to lend
Everyone needs good neighbours, without them, where would we be?
In a wee place like Harburn, they're one big family

So all that remains, I think, to say
Is many congratulations on your Silver Wedding Anniversary
With a bit of luck, there'll be another do twenty five years from now
Let's see, that'll be me about ninety-eight, I might just make it
    somehow

To Sandra and Eric, good luck, long life, good health and God bless
Thank you for letting us share tonight's celebrations
Here's to you both – a' the best

24 November 1998

Sarah & Will's Wedding Day

It's Sarah and Will's wedding, what can I say?
At this moment in time, it is a happy day
Surrounded by family to help launch the happy pair
They're on the crest of a wave, the weather set fair

Will, as I know him, is a genuine chap
He knows where he is going, there's no doubting that
He aims to do it his way, with help from no man
And good on you, Wills, if you believe in yourself
You can do it, you can

As for Sarah, she'll always be Sarah, all she wants out of life
Is to be married, have a family, be a mother and wife
After all, that's what the good Lord intended since the beginning
    of time
As it was in the beginning, still nature defines

So to them both as on life's journey they now embark
My advice is to be patient, be tolerant, never lose heart
Life's sometimes not easy, but with someone by your side
You'll overcome anything, each storm over-ride

I wish Sarah and Will good luck and God bless
The future is in your own hands, I know you'll both do your best

29 August 1998

Happy Days at Braehead Burn

I let my mind go on a journey
Doon memory lane tae days gone by
When wi' the weans, we'd go on a picnic
Tae listen for the cuckoo, watch the skylark soar up high

I'd spread ma mither's auld plaid on the banking
While the weans here and there did run
Laid the basket wi' the jammy pieces doon beside it
Stuck a bottle of juice securely in the burn

It was so quiet and peaceful, apart frae the laughter o' the weans
As they ran back an' forth across the auld iron bridge
An' the splashes as they threw the stanes
Gowans, buttercups and daisy smells – and sounds of countryside
Birds, bees and butterflies paint a picture to recall in later life

They could safely run roon anywhere, dae anything they liked
Nae transistors in those days, nae skateboards or mountain bikes
A ball and bat, a bow and arrow made wi' a rowan twig and string
A piece of wood for a wee boat and auld rope for a Tarzan swing

Around them grazed the sheep and cattle, tails swinging to and fro
In the hedges they discovered an empty blackie's nest an' at the
    tap of the tree, a crow's
Somewhere in the distance, they could hear a peewee cry
And whiles among the marsh marigolds, they'd glimpse a dragonfly

I'd sit there and meditate while they paddled in the burn
Busy building a dookin' hole, then in bare skud they'd run
For a while that kept them happy, then they'd think o' anither ploy
A game o' rounders this time, the girls against the boys

Or a game o' cowboys and Indians, in and oot among the trees
Crawling on their bellies and on their hands and knees
Soon they would begin to feel hungry and wi' a jam piece
    in each haun'
They'd run further doon tae look for minnows an' make mud pies
    in a can

Sometimes a squabble would arise o'er some wee silly thing
Someone had someone else's jar or pinched a bit o' string
Soon they'd show signs o' tiredness, time tae make oor way
    back hame
There were nae mair jelly pieces left and they'd tired o' playing games

As they toddled doon the road, sunburned tae a crisp
The lassies pulling cuckoo flowers, the laddies looking for pud-
    docks in the ditch
They'd throw them at the lassies, an' make them howl wi' fright
An' they'd throw sticky-willy back, then run wi' a' their might

Nae need for bedtime stories that night, they were sleeping
    on their feet
Leaving Ma and Pa in peace and quiet, these times were hard to beat

26 May 1999

Christmas

Christmas is drawing nearer, there's no escaping that
There's brochures popping through the letterbox, landing on the mat
Book World telling you you could win five thousand pounds
    in the great free draw
If you purchase any of their many books on fishing, golfing or fitba'

Damart send a catalogue, now winter's here to stay
Saying valued customers get a free gift if you order in time
    for Christmas Day
Britannia offering you the very latest CD
No obligation to buy, try them first, and to your home address
    fast delivery

Rangers Club, their latest gear through your letter box arrives
New strip, scarf, football boots etc. The price! You can't believe
    your eyes!
Pamphlets saying, Go on, treat yourself to the latest mobile phone
Forget crowded shops and queues, let BT Cellnet do your shopping
    straight from home

Homebase promises great value from Christmas trees to Santa
    and his sleigh
Led by Rudolph the red-nosed reindeer, children's favourite
    to this day
Craft fairs, sales of work, bazaars wherever there is space
Santas, snowmen by the score, which ever way you gaze

Outings to the theatre and pantomime, put your name down if you'd
    like to go
Christmas cards in aid of charity, Save the Children, Christian Aid
    and Dr Barnardo

Pamphlets from Farmfoods, Iceland, Asda and Safeway
Advertising their many goodies saying, Buy one, get one free

Christmas carols, Jingle Bells, Ding Dong Merrily on High
Ring out in every shop and supermarket when you go in to buy
I'm just an OAP with X-amount of cash
Doing my very best each week to try and make it last

I've none of thae credit cards, you know, all made of plastic
And my pension, sad to say, isn't made like elastic
As Christmas comes, lest we forget, what it really means to us all –
Peace on earth, goodwill to all mankind, the baby Jesus
   in a manger stall

It's all so commercialised now, one big spending spree
We're all about collapsing by the time the needles fall off
   the Christmas tree

1999

Mary Maclaughlan's 50th Birthday
& 30th Wedding Anniversary

Mary made her debut into the world on August fifteenth
    nineteen-forty-nine
The ambulance driver breaking the speed limit
To get her mum and dad into Edinburgh on time
I always thought she was born before they got there
But I'm told that wasnae true, they made it with just minutes to spare

Tam, being a good shepherd, could have handled the birthing
    coolly and calmly
For both man and beast, since the beginning of time
Enter and leave the world the same way
So all's well that ends well, it came to pass
May and Tam were now the parents of a bonnie wee lass

They brought her hame to Ormiston Farm Cottage before moving
    to Harburnhead
And like all the new born, soon thrived very quickly, she slept
    and was fed
That was in the days of free orange juice, cod liver oil and
    national dried milk
Maybe that had something to do wi' her rich, coppery red hair
That always shimmered like silk

When she was just a toddler, Tam taen a herding at Stanhope
An idyllic spot by the Tweed
Surrounded by rolling hills, you got across to the house
    via a staunch wooden bridge
I can picture it yet, we visited them there quite a few times
Sheep an' lambs as far as the eye could see, the summers were fine
But the winters must hae been lonely

Mary's playmates were a collection of four-legged friends
Sandy her favourite cairn, five or six working collies o' her faither's
Twa cats, no' forgetting the hens

Then school days were looming ever closer
They decided to come back to Harburn once more
From Torphin Cottage she walked tae the auld school
Just a stane's throw frae the door

Then frae there tae the auld Cauther High afore it moved to Polbeth
A model pupil was she
A budding pianist an' a' if she'd continued
But it was que sera sera – what will be will be
Allan had arrived on the scene, ye ken whit I mean, he upset
    the whole applecart
It was goodbye to *doh-ray-me and soh-fah-lah*
    with auld Airchie Russell and Mrs McGrath

Oh, it was good fun, it always is when you're young
They said, They're schoolkids yet
For the moment we'll leave them alone, it'll soon fizzle oot, I bet

But devil the fear, you couldn't part the pair
They stuck together through thick and thin
They travelled on the red Lanark bus everyday
Back and forth to college, her and him

It was now nineteen-sixty-eight, the strain was proving
    too great
It cramped their style courting 'en route', you could say
And I'm telling you, it caused a hullaballoo before the pair o' them
    at last got their way

They married in the West Kirk on a bitterly cauld January day
Before coming up to this very hall

The only method of heating you up was the auld pot-bellied stove
Plus twa or three haufs o' the best guaranteed, to keep oot the cauld

It was an auld-fashioned wedding, Michael and I were baith there
Hooching awa' to Jim Todd's dance band
The bride an' groom left about midnight but had to turn back
    at Burnwynde
The key o' their flat was still wi' their best man

The honeymoon weekend went by in a flash
They slept in on Monday, Allan had to make a mad dash
You see, that morn he had to sit his final examination
He missed the first part, he lost so many marks
I wonder what they thought about his explanation

A year later, many changes around by their first anniversary
Allan graduates, gets a new job, a new hoose in Livingston, and, oh
    happy day!
They announce the glad tidings to the whole of the street
That they would soon hear the patter of two tiny feet

Umpteen problems arose, but they got them ironed oot
And when Andrew arrived, it was a case o' like mother like son
He couldna wait to get oot
A grandson to love and adore for Tam and May
They took him to Glenluce, his first caravan holiday
While Mary and Allan ventured on a Wallace Arnold bus to Austria
    for their first trip abroad
Mary now decides not to go back to college but to get a job

Another move, this time they buy their first hoose in Dedridge Row
They change this, change that, renovate and enlarge it and after
    two years have it just so
When Allan applies for a post in an approved school, in Aberdeen
    this time

Mary starts wi' the Hydro Board, where for thirteen years
    shall we say Mrs M is in her prime

Allan, wi' Mary's support, does an Open University degree
She sits up half the night, plying him wi' numerous sandwiches
    and large mugs o' coffee and tea
It certainly paid off, promotion wisna' long in coming
Well, you ken the auld saying, behind every successful man
    you'll find a guid woman

Tam, by this time, had given up herding sheep and started herding
    weans
He was born too early, Tam was a wise man, aye, he used his brains
When Andrew first started school, it was every five year old's dream
His grandad was the janny who was held in high esteem

Time moves on, Mary's made redundant, no' needed ony mair
She gets a job as a dental receptionist and starts a brand new career
She also thinks it's aboot time tae learn tae drive
Three years later she passes first time after one hundred
    and twenty four lessons
Tae mak' it rhyme I'll add wan and call it twenty five

They celebrated their Silver Wedding wi' a family doo at Harburn
    big hoose
Andrew graduates as a vet and is now able to tell you, in medical
    terms, whit's wrang wi' yer cat, dog or moose
I gather he is a man o' a great many talents
But at this moment in time, he keeps himself busy
    playing the braw gallant

Mary hopes some time in the future, he'll maybe settle doon
She'd like tae be a granny afore it's possible tae holiday on the moon

For they've been everywhere else recently, it's the only place left
    tae go
I gathered that frae Allan's notes – isn't that so?

Home for them noo is a two-hundred-year-auld farmhoose
    at Harrit Mains
I was mairrit frae there, but, oh, my, how it's changed
The dairy too, is someone's home sweet home
There's another hoose in tae the left and the auld round shed
    has gone
Also an upmarket hoose, yon muckle barn where they stored
    a' the grain
There's naewhere noo tae plank yer bike for a snog in oot o' the
    rain

I'm nearing the end of this saga Allan asked me tae dae
A rather long ode to Mary on her fiftieth birthday
I've enjoyed reminiscing, the pleasure was mine
Many happy returns of the day, Mary
I hope your dreams for the future come true
I'm sure that they will – given time

Jean Graham – 70th Birthday

What can one say about Jean?
For a start, she's got that many freens
To invite them all you'd need the Usher Hall
And it was booked for tonight, so it seems

They say that she's seventy today, I can hardly believe it, no way
She gets up with the lark, feeds calves, dogs and cats
That's the way she starts off the day

195

Once that job's over, she jumps in the Land Rover
With Andra, her eldest son
Goes the rounds, counting the beasts
To see they're hale and hearty at least
And there's no' any went on the run

She must have a timetable pinned on the wa'
To see where she goes next and who for
She never says no, she just up and goes
Half the folk here rely on Jean and her car

She visits the sick and the lame
If you're housebound and left on your ain
She'll go to the Co-op, nothing's a bother, you know
The chemist, or Asda for Michael's fags when he's nane

She gives out wheelchairs for the Red Cross
Drives the elderly folk to and from Stewart Court
Turns up when needed, without fail, and tells them a tale
O' her brother-in-law Wullie's in-growing toenail

At the Rural or up at the West Church
Ye'll see her pourin' out tea or else washing up
She never hurries away, it being Sunday
She's no' in such a rush

At baking she's got what it takes
Especially her pineapple cakes
She does the farm books and VAT
She'll lend you a hat
For a wedding or whatever it takes

Her grandweans, before they learned to drive
Would phone and ask could she pick them up before five?

Saying, I've got to be doon the road before my mother gets back
Or she's sure to skin me alive

In the winter she fills her time
At the rink curling, she's a great curler, mind
In Harburn drama group she excels
Although she'd no' say so hersel'
She's far too modest and kind

She's been on the Dairy Maids committee for years
Bid a fond farewell to quite a few of the dears
She's still in it today, long may she continue, I say
And so say all of us here

Myself, I would be lost without Jean
For many years she's been a great freen
I see her nearly every day, and I mean what I say
Where would we all be without Jean?

1 September 2002

The Aga

The much-longed for event took place, on a cold January morn
An easterly wind, blowing in from the sea, heralding a storm
It was ten in the morning, when my wish it was granted
I'd dreamed of this moment for years, the only thing I'd ever wanted

It transformed our home, it still remains in my mind
We immediately bonded and celebrated with a glass of red wine
As I gazed at the new addition to our home, I was completely ga-ga
And, no, it wasn't a new baby, it was my navy blue Aga

It reminded me of home, my father and mother
Surrounded by comfort and love, my sisters and brothers
Standing in the kitchen, never going out summer or winter
Drying out clothes on the rail, opening the oven
To see what was for dinner

The kettle always boiling away, ready for a cuppa
Pancakes, just newly baked, ready to spread on the butter
Warming our hands, coming in from the cold
Getting out of our gladrags and on with the old

Leaning against it to ease a sore tummy
In a way, it comforted you just like a mummy
Family conferences held, in its stately presence
Problems discussed, worries quickly were lessened

Always there in good times or in bad
If you haven't an Aga it's high time you had
It's there for a lifetime, there when you need it
It hears all, sees all and keeps many a secret

You're relaxed by its warmth, it's a bit like the sun
It's always around but it weighs half a ton!

January 1999

A Millennium Celebration – The West Kirk

When asked tae write a verse or two
For tonight's get-together wi' friends baith auld and new
I thought, Now, how will I start?
Having lived for many years well off the beaten track
And living in the country, you could say

The Kirk was often miles away
Nae motor car tae get you there and back, jist your ain two fit
Encased in sturdy shoes, and of course, your Sunday hat

The first time I attended Sunday Schule
Twas in a wee auld hut, I mind it still
A man frae the Kirk came on his bike
Telt bible stories tae a' the weans, Catholic and Protestant alike
It's probably the only stories some got telt
Before bedtime they'd mair than likely get a skelp

The hall was full, for in those bygone days
They tended tae hae large families
And if you attended faithfully
You received a wee text before you went away
Adorned wi' flowers of every hue
Sometimes wi' Jesus in a robe of blue
Beautifully penned saying, God is love, I am the light, I am the way
I still remember it to this day

Time moved on, folks got married once they'd grown up
Nearly always in the home or hall, the manse, very rarely
    in the church
Six o'clock, Friday nights, that was then the norm
The weekly toil over, nae work or early rise next morn

The weans, of course, soon came along, by this time
    usually three or four
You'd be that busy caring for your brood, you hardly ever crossed
    the door

But there was aye the young folk's guild in Stewart Street Hall
It helped to keep you sane
Meetings, dances, drama group, jumble sales

Concerts, fun and games
Cupid, when passing by, frae time tae time dropped in
For his usual game of darts, sometimes he lost, sometimes he'd win

Sunday Schule held in the Kirk itself, six groups meant six teachers
     tae
Upstairs, doonstairs, in every corner, wee groups of weans nearly
     every Sunday
Sunday Schule trips to Aberdour, Burntisland, gie often marred
     by rain
Singing, Peas And Beans And Barley O', in a wee Kirk Hall in Biggar
Was I no' thankful when the bus arrived
Tae take us all back hame

Then, of course, the weans were christened in the Kirk
Wrapped tightly in Granny's haun'-knitted shawl
How proud you were tae see their names added tae the cradle roll
The Nativity play was sometimes performed by adults successfully
     I might say
Michael once played the part of Joseph and Ann Brash
     was a sweet Mary

I even scrubbed the Kirk wi' my mother once
When Davie and Mrs Calder they were stuck
Doon on ma hauns and knees for hours, when finished, I couldna
     straighten up

And I've heard it said, before I was born
That the Kirk bells tolled thrice on a Sunday
First at eight o'clock tae say
Do you know what day it is today?
Come on, get up you sleepy head
Get washed and dressed, eat your ham an' eggs

Then again at ten and twelve they tolled loud and clear
Telling all, Doors open now, come, you're welcome here

You were meant tae keep the Sabbath day for rest and prayer
    no work and play
An' woe betide you if you hung oot yer claes, it was frowned upon
    even in my days

WEST KIRK of CALDER

Come tae think of it, you'd even on a Sunday, tae hae a cauld high-tea
Don't make a noise, and behave yourself, oh, dearie me!

Well, there you are, I've done my bit
A humble servant of the auld parish Kirk
And it's left me thinking, isn't life strange?
It's aye been there for me, it's now even in my name

February 2000

Rabbie the Conservationist

Way back in your day, Rabbie
As you followed your horse and plough
You were a conservationist
And thought as we do now

It troubled you the plight o' yon wee moose
When you unwittingly demolished its wee hoose
You showed even then your concern
For the humble daisy, moose an' fern
In the race to progress we get carried away
An' you're no' gonna believe the things that are happening the day

We're into another decade and lucky so far
We're still on Planet Earth, and fleein' about in our cars
But they say we're gradually going doon the hill
Nature's balance, they're telling us, will soon be nil
God forbid they cannot foresee

That the stuff they're disposing of in the air and sea
Are endangering all our earthly species
And we'll be next if it increases

Oor climate the noo is upside doon
We've had gales and floods, it's like the monsoon
They've got Voyager up there the noo, sussing things oot
To see if there's a planet somewhere that will sustain life
Before this one's caput

In the ozone layer they've found a hole
Somewhere in the Arctic region near the Pole
Let's hope, as they say, a stitch in time
They'll be able to mend it, an' we'll a' be fine
Oor planet, they say, is overheating
Rainforests are disappearing and wildlife retreating

Oor rivers tae are clear nae mair
The puir wee fish are short o' air
The seas an' a' are no' exempt
They're a' polluted tae some extent

Wild flowers I used to pu' as a wean
Are vanishing an' a' – where hae they gaen?
I ken folks' gardens are right braw
But the flowers o' the countryside were there for a'

Some of the animals roon the globe
Will soon be extinct, it's an awfy job
By destroying their natural habitat
They are gradually disappearing aff the map

And trees that have stood for generations
Are made into nappies for the younger population

Paper hankies, toilet rolls and towels
Friends Of The Earth, it makes them howl

Mind, I sometimes buy these items noo masel'
They are in the shops, so I might as well
I must admit, it bothers me
So I buy recycled ones, you see

Ony bottles of Aqua we consume
To the bottle bank I take them doon
Progress, well, some things are nice
But it seems, of course, it has its price

We're living longer noo, they say
And night comes after a much extended day
We've this and that to cure oor ills
Blood pressure tablets, water pills
Yes, it seems we're all much better aff
Mair able to tred a longer path

I'm sure, Rabbie, the complaint that cut you doon
Could have been rectified the day if you'd still been aroon

Then again, as you believed in living life to the full
You wouldn'na hae appreciated it once your ardour had cooled

I must admit there have been great strides
Positive changes on every side
Folk are beginning I think to realise
The need to pull the gither tae survive

You said yourself that man to man
Would brothers be across all lands
It's coming yet, is what you said
The world o'er, all grudges fade
Well, your prophecies are coming true
Just look what's happening the noo

East and West are shaking hands, exchanging felicitations
The winds of change are blowing
But it will take a lot of time and patience
So let's hope the powers that be on this green planet will see
    the light in time
An' get us back on an even keel for the sake o' a' mankind

An' there's always tomorrow, things never bide the same
Times are aye changing, an' there's aye the weans
Coming up wi' new ideas, putting wrongs tae right
I just hope I live to see it... you just never know, I might
So, Rabbie, here's tae oor wee planet earth, I'm sure there is no other
Oot there in the galaxy – so let's treat her kindly – jist like oor mother

Summer 2000

What have I got up to this summer?
It seems to have gone by in a flash
I haven't been to the seaside
To watch the waves roll in the splash

I've spent it at home picking berries
Making jam from the fruits of the earth
Went a few bus trips with old friends
Viewing the Scottish countryside at its best

I've watched family and friends go off
To Cyprus, Italy and Spain
Heard how their flights were delayed for hours
They were dead tired when they arrived back hame

The folk up the road went to Turkey
The temperature soared sky-high
They'd to stay inside two days running
They, of course, went in the middle of July

The couple next door went with their in-laws
There was a mix-up when they arrived at the hotel
They spent the first night coupled up together
Which didn't go down very well

Things got fixed out in the long run
They were moved to another room nearby
Alas, there was no air conditioning
An electric fan they had to go out and buy

My eldest went white-water rafting
Down the Colorado River – in the latest designer shorts
Got badly burnt in the process
The sun was so very hot

Another I know went to Lanzarote
And didn't see the sun for a week
The shamal blew a wind from the desert
While at home we basked in sunshine and heat

I've seen snapshots of folk paragliding
Lazing by the pool in bikinis and such
Sporting expensive sunglasses, etcetera
Some topless on the beach – makes me blush

So I've no holiday photos to show you
No hair-raising tales to relate
But it's only the third of September
Who knows? As they say, it's never too late

Burns Night – Harburn Hall

Weel, Rabbie, dear, another year
Oor annual get-together
I promised you last year if I was still around
I would keep the date, come hail, rain, wind or weather

Back amang auld freens and acquaintances in this year
    two thousand and one
Where I first paid you homage, in this very hall, by reciting
Tae a Moose by Burns

If your birthday had been in December
The invite I wid hae tae hae declined
As I was doon in St John's CCU, a' wired up
Feeling anything but fine

But wi' a' the latest techniques and drugs plus a' the TLC
I've got back on an even keel
In time tae tell you aboot
Last year's Burns Supper in Burnhouse Skule

Burnhouse Skule Burns' Supper – 2000

Last January in Burnhouse Skule – they held a Burns' Supper
A wilder night they couldn'a hae picked, a force ten gale was blawin'
    the rain runnin' doon the gutters
Guests beginnin' tae arrive, the company near completed
When somebody pointed out, a veggie haggis wis urgently needed
Weel, of course, they hadn'a thought o' that, it hadn'a crossed
    their mind
That some folk might object to sup oor national dish
Oor wholesome haggis abhorrent find

So Mary had tae dae a U-turn, back tae Harrit Mains
Get ane oot her freezer an' hurry back again
Ane man's meat is anither's poison, so I have heard it say
I'm shair that problem never would have arisen back in Rabbie's day

The veggie haggis duly arrived, though dished up a wee bit late
I bet they never wid hae kent the difference, unless it had been
    served on different plates
The piper when he piped it in, a mention he does merit
I think he wid hae been mair in tune, if he'd squeezed a bag o' ferrets

It seemed the piper went ootside
Tae gie his pipes a practice blaw
Atmospheric changes played havoc wi' his reeds
Just as he made his entrance tae the ha'

The haggis was proudly borne aloft by Dave
Whose surname to pronounce I dare not try
But for a' that he was born a Scotsman
An' a Scotsman he expects to die

Allan then got up tae address the humble haggis
Wi' rusty knife in haun', he really looked quite savage
His bushy beard, his Maclaughlan kilt, big bare knees
I swear I heard the puir wee thing plead, o' please!

Do the deed, mak' it quick an' clean – dinna mak a hash o' it
But Allan, sorry to say
Forgot tae sharp his trusty blade that day

He had tae strike the haggis twice – the bum
Guid job he wisnae there at Bannockburn

A tribute tae the Bard's Immortal Memory
Was ably given by Mr Bill Gourlay
I'll drop the mister and ca' him Bill
He delivered his speech wi' the greatest skill

Fu' marks tae the great man – ten oot o' ten
You'll see, they'll ask him back again
Being heidie o' a neighbouring schule
The honour he was mair than able tae fulfil

Then Bella Kirk in broad Scots tongue
Telt a few o' her stories, kept a date wi' Burns
According tae Jim and Allan, it went doon well
A pat on the back for oor wee Bell

As for Jim, whit can I say? He was so efficient, oozing charm an'
     vitality
Reciting Tam O' Shanter, ne'er looking at a page
While at the same time showing us on the screen – the bold Tammy's
     escapades
In shirt an' tartan trews, as he passed me by
I thought, jist the very lad to meet a bonnie lass while coming
     through the rye

A toast tae the lassies was brawly tackled by Tom Lee
Who, once he had his say aboot the fairer sex
Passed wi' flying colours
If no' an A most certainly a B

The reply was given by Alison
And, weel, whit can I say?
The lady got her point ower, wi' the help o' a hoover, etc
She certainly did it her way

They hooched an' danced whiles in between
Had a sang or twa frae Elizabeth, Jim's auld schule freen
She sang so sweetly, almost wi' a haunting air
Aboot a lass left wi' a newborn babe
Wondering who'd buy the bairn cloots tae wear

Also John Lindsay resplendent in his new kilt and sporran
Gave us My Love is Like a Red, Red Rose
His tenor voice in excellent form

The Reverend McCracken gied us The Selkirk Grace
An' ended the proceedings wi' a vote o' thanks
Afore we a' went oor separate ways

So Burnhouse's first Burns' Supper was voted a great success
An' they've a' been eagerly lookin' forrit tae this ane
So let's see if we can make Harburn Burns Supper – Simply The Best

This auld army hut, past its best an' showin' signs o' wear and tear
Can still attract folk frae a' walks of life, yes – frae baith far and near
So Allan and the Rural Men have proved their efforts were
    well worthwhile
An' John's caricature of Tammy belting across the Whistle Brig
Surely wid ha' made oor Rabbie smile

April Fool

I had a little hen, it had a wooden leg
The best little hen that ever laid an egg
I took it to the farmer, who lived up at the farm
When he saw it, he said, My goodness, I'll be darned!
I've never seen the like in all my life
Put it with the other hens, while I go and tell the wife
Come and see what I've got, he begged
I've a little brown hen with a wooden leg
Coming dear! she called, This I've got to see!
To find it was a joke, a huntegowk, ha-ha-ha-hee-hee!

January 2001

Neighbourhood Watch

Spring must surely be arriving soon
From my window I can see
Two stock doves sitting on the telephone wires
As close as close can be
Enjoying the lovely sunshine
After the dreadful winter weather
Cooing softly to each other
Preening each other's feathers

I think they must be courting
As I sit and watch and wait
I gather he's made up his mind
He'd like her for his mate
There they are, they're getting amorous
He's giving her a peck
Followed by another and another
As they sit there neck to neck

They seem to prefer the telephone cable
Now, I wonder why
Maybe they get an extra buzz
On that tightrope in the sky

Now they're getting fidgety, I think
They sense they're being watched
They move to the nearby sycamore tree
Sitting very near the top

They're eyeing up a row of conifers
Which divide our house from the old manse next door

Perhaps in which to build a love nest
For two or three or four

They've flown over for a closer look
Hopping from branch to branch
Swaying gently in the breeze
In a rock-and-roll sort of dance

They seem to be viewing the area
Definitely interested in the site
Making sure it's suitable
Wind and watertight

Safe from marauding magpies
From past experience they know too well
They really are a menace
Neighbours straight from hell

Now the two of them have flown away
Much to my great sorrow
My entertainment over for the day
Perhaps they'll come back tomorrow

Maybe they've other sites to view
Somewhere where there's more privacy
Away from noisy neighbours and traffic fumes
More environmentally friendly

They could have flown up to Harburn
Keen for a taste of the good life
Maybe his mate fancies a more up-market area
Beside the gentry she wants to bide
I've no' seen them for a day or two
The weather's to blame, I think – grey skies instead of blue

A week went by before they finally did appear
I'm almost sure it's the same two, last week's courting pair
They must have decided to settle in Hartwood Road
Think it's safer where they'll feel more at hame
You know, up there at Harburn
Someone might have ta'en a potshot at them

They could have ended up on the menu
At the Club House, or Cannons Restaurant à la carte
I think they maybe made a wise decision
And I'm glad they've both come back
It's nice to see them to-ing and fro-ing
Everything going to plan
Just one move from they thieving magpies
Neighbourhood Watch is there to lend a helping hand

March 2000

Yvonne & Adam's Wedding

Dear Elizabeth and Ian, I'm writing to say
We were honoured, indeed, to be there at Yvonne and Adam's big day
We'd a wonderful time, blessed with good weather
A real Scottish theme throughout, kilts, piper, thistles and heather

Things couldn't have gone any better, however hard you tried
Two bonnie bridesmaids and a beautiful bride
The gasps of admiration, from out of the guests
When they glimpsed the happy couple
Adam resplendent in full Highland dress

Elizabeth, you were a picture, there's no doubting that
What an excellent choice of colour – that dress and that hat!

Ian in his tartan kilt, so proud, there by your side
Two wonderful parents beaming with pride

The wedding service over, a guard of honour awaited as they came
    into view
The comments from the waiting crowd as they tried to get through
Then off to the reception, while we the guests followed on
A photo session followed outside on the lawn

An excellent meal came next – definitely à la carte
Everything going as planned – right from the start
Efficient service throughout from the staff at the Strathaven Hotel
Champagne, no less, to toast the bride and bridesmaids'
    happiness and health

We then mingled and chatted, until the dancing began
The atmosphere, one of great happiness, was helped by a truly
    great band
Michael says to tell you since coming back hame
After seeing these two dolly birds, he's no' been the same

Their singing, their dress and movements, as they sang Waterloo
Put his blood pressure at a dangerous level, but thankfully
    it's back to normal noo
He's never stopped talking about your three lovely lassies
He hopes he's still around for the next doo, for mind
    time quickly passes

Anyway, you'll have gathered by now we're very happy to say
Thanks to you both for a really great day
PS: I'm sure the photographs – once they're processed
Could grace the Hello Magazine – they'll be simply The Best

14 August 2000

Home on the Range

I'm dreaming of home and the days that are gone
I see the fire in the auld kitchen range
The weans washed and fed in the auld boxed-in bed
Wi' a sigh I think how time's changed

CHORUS

Home aroon the auld range
The kettle is singing away
The cat's asleep by the fire
I pile the logs up higher
Oh, for those happy auld days

I say, Cuddle doon there in bed
Till I get ma Red Letter read
Then I think of what I hae tae dae
There's socks to be darned
Working claes tae be warmed
Laid oot by the fire for next day

The auld man's asleep in his chair
Dreaming away his cares
Tomorrow will bring what it may
All's quiet, not a sound, as I look roon the room
I can see the auld rag rugs on the flair

I see the auld rows, their auld brick wa's
The reek fae their fires oot the lum
Claes blowing away on a guid summer's day
The relief when the day's work was done

I sit there and dream aboot auld neighbours and freens
Aye there if you needed them
They'd say come on ben wi' me
We'll hae a wee cup of tea
And a blether, you'll feel better then

How times have changed like the auld kitchen range
They're in the past noo, where they belong
But fond memories stay, you can't take them away
They keep coming back, like an old song

Déjà Vu

A severe weather warning had been issued saying snow was on
    the way
Sweeping across the country turning the sky a dark and murky grey
The birds must have known by instinct or by some uncanny
    sixth-sense
They'd suddenly all disappeared from the trees behind
    the garden fence

It wasn't long before the first snowflakes silently floated down
Getting larger and faster as they swirled and twirled around
Till billions and trillions of snowflakes seemed to fill the air
Blotting out the landscape, they were everywhere

The wind got up, it became a blizzard and continued through
    the night
It swept across the countryside turning everything to white
It was as if nature had decided it was time for a spring clean
Every imperfection, every blemish was gone leaving everything
    fresh and pure, it seemed

You awoke to an eerie silence suggesting something was amiss
Drew back the bedroom curtains saying, Come and look at this
The snow had stopped by this time, the sky a lovely blue
I gazed at this calm and tranquil scene with a sense of déjà vu

That year it had been snowing heavily for days, roads completely
    blocked
Food stocks running out, both for the shepherd and his flock
Michael had been staying at Harrit with my mother as he couldn't
    get home from work
He knew about these conditions, they could last for weeks
They'd been snowed in many times in the past
And things like oatmeal and flour forever wouldn't last
They would have plenty of logs and peat for the fire to keep warm
    at night
But without oil for the lamps there'd be no shining light

His boss's brother, also from farming stock, agreed to accompany him
Try and take up some provisions, tobacco for his father, for his
    mother paraffin
The laird of Harrit Mains, kindly offered the farm's two Clydesdales
They set off on their journey, hoping they wouldn't fail

They got the length of Turniemoon on their great adventure
Found the snow was up to the horse's belly no further could
    they venture
Michael's partner had to turn back with the horses, while he
    continued on
His journey of mercy, see if he could make it on his own

The road, although impassable, the snow had frozen solid as a rock
He found to his amazement he could walk on top
He must have felt like Jesus walking on the waters, and well he might
As he made it up to Crosswoodburn where he stayed the night

Next day, he made his way back to Harrit, at Harburn the mist
    came down
He completely lost his bearings, he seemed in circles to go around
At last he came across a derelict farmhouse where he sheltered
    in the barn
There was a pile of straw in the corner where some old tramp
    had lain to keep warm

At times, he'd been only yards from the Bog Burn
And as the crow flies, two miles from Cobbinshaw loch
He must have been following someone's invisible footsteps
    or maybe someone's ghost

In his knapsack he had a dozen new-laid eggs for his future
    mother-in-law
He made a hole and sucked three of them before lying down
    in the straw
He couldn't sleep but stayed there in that big empty barn
It wasn't till later he found out that was where I was born

Kiprig

After an hour or two, the mist lifted, it was now bright and clear
As he walked, he saw the lights on top of Addiewell bing
    he had nothing now to fear
He followed that guiding light until he came to Harrit Mains
Needless to say, he was so relieved and thankful he'd come
    to his journey's end

He was off work for a fortnight with exhaustion
    and a housemaid's knee
The snow lay on the roadside that year well into the month of May
We were married in the September for he vowed he never
    would again
Travel that road in the winter, no' even in the rain

That was fifty-four years ago and the snowstorm was nature's way
Of reminding us, lest we forget, just how awesome it can be

1 March 2001

Tae a Dumplin'

We're a' weel-versed on the haggis
That great Scottish dish
When partaken wi' tatties an' neeps
Alang wi' a dram, they say, is pure bliss
We toast it, salute it, in a' kinds o' tongues
In January each year as we pay homage tae Burns

But there's another Scottish dish deserving o' praise
It graced mony a table, back in the auld days
At weddings, christenings, birthdays where ere

There was a need to celebrate
Amang the sausage rolls an' egg sannies
It took pride o' place

If you've no' guessed whit it is, I'll enlighten you a'
It's roon', got a smooth outer skin, a bit like a fitba'
The auld clootie dumplin', still a favourite today
Eaten straight frae the pot, hot or cauld, ony which way

At Hogmanay it soaks up the whisky
Afore it gets tae yer heid
It's nice fried wi' a guid bit o' ham, a fresh egg
An' a slice o' store breid

An' whit does it consist o', this great delicacy?
Weel, there's floor, currants an' raisins, syrup, treacle
Ginger and cinnamon spice tae
I aye add a grated apple an' carrot then milk and an egg
Some folks though prefer chopped orange peel instead

Wrapped in greaseproof paper, you put some trinkets
    an' a siller threepenny bit
A button, a thimble, horseshoe, a ring, a wee china doll are a' put
    in the mix
If ye got a thimble, an auld maid ye were destined tae be
A button meant you'd remain a bachelor free
The ring for a weddin', a horseshoe guid luck
A china doll, a new baby, the siller threepenny you'd come intae
    money
Perhaps your coupon wad come up

Then up on the stove goes the big iron pot
Three quarters fu' o' biling water, you then dip in your cloth
Lay out flat on the table, spread liberally wi' flour
Gather and tie tightly wi' string an' bile for three or four hours

The cloth is very important – it must be linen or cotton
A large dish cloth or pillowslip, nothing man-made for a dumplin'
    that's not on
Material that'll allow the mixture tae breathe and tae swell
Like a pregnant woman, it requires regular check-ups
Tae mak' shair it's progressing well

See that it's kept boiling, don't let it go aff the boil
Or a' yer hard work will shairly be spoiled
You don't want a soggy mess that'll leave you wi' heartburn
Keep topping the pot up wi' boiling water – if ye think that it
    needs some

Once the time has elapsed, tak it oot o' the pot
Watch, don't burn yer fingers, it's extremely hot
Afore untying the string, pour over a jug o' cauld watter
Carefully peel off the cloth an' transfer tae a platter

There it is, a perfect clootie dumplin'
Lookin' an' smellin' simply divine
Noo, where's the pairty?
At your hoose or mine?

June 2001

Remembering Rena

As we remember Rena, she came from a large family
With her many brothers and sisters, school days flew by
Quite different to those of today
At fourteen she left school, stopped playing peavers an' bools
Down to the Grant's Bake Hoose she went
To learn the auld trade, hoo a hauf loaf was made
Strange how some things are meant

An' she learned fast, I would say, rolls and scones by the tray
Cream buns and strawberry cakes by the score
So it was easy to see when she got a break for her tea
She'd hae a vanilla slice that had somehow fell on the floor

Then along came Danny in his jaunty red tammy
A paratrooper dashing and brave
They very soon married, had two lads an' three lassies
He was a good carpenter too, it was said

225

Her time in the bakehoose stood her in good stead
She was a dab-hand at the baking – cherry cake and shortbread
Aye, she was a great mother, likewise to Danny a wife
You could always rely on Rena, she got by
On the bare necessities of life

She was a one-off, quite unique, a weel-kent face in the street
Made welcome wherever she went
She was as bright as a bee, aye reminded me
Wi' her five chickens o' a prood, wee bantam hen

She was a bundle of fun – ladies' nights she helped run
Wi' a few auld freens like hersel'

Rena and Bella as Fran and Anna

She'd sing her auld songs, in a voice good and strong
The applause she got spoke for itsel'

She travelled to Canada back and forth, tae Ireland, of course
Once to Russia wi' a freen, by mini bus
She loved a run by the Clyde, a game o' bingo besides
Aye, Rena was just one o' us

Noo, I'm almost shuir, she's somewhere up there
Gie'n them Bonnie Wee Jeannie McCall
An' Maggie Cocky Bendy for an encore
As she's done many times, in this very hall

March 2003

Wullie & Myra's Golden Wedding

When Wullie and Myra got married, I wasn't there
Michael was his best man, Wullie paid his fare
I stayed at home with Michael and John
But am honoured to be here tonight, fifty years on

Sadly, by myself, but that's how life goes
I'm sure Michael's here with us in spirit, who knows?
Tonight I'd like to focus on a young English lass
Whom I've got to know over the years
How quickly time's flown past

When Wullie met Myra she was just seventeen
He fell for her hook, line and sinker, she was the girl of his dreams
She was tall and slender as a willow branch
The bonniest lass there that night at the dance

They were wed when Myra reached the age of eighteen
He flew wi' her up ower the border, far from her large family
    and freens
She must have been homesick many a time
No phone in those days to let folks know she was getting on fine

A room and kitchen in Stewart Street was their first nest site
An outside loo and wash-house, an' that fire!
Myra could never get it to light
An' a trip to the loo, the only one in the block
It was used by four houses, she often found the door locked

Her efforts to become domesticated, I'm telling you
She was the first to admit she hadna a clue
Her first pot of soup Wullie will always remember
Coming home from his work one cold, wet November
She generously served it, out of the pot
Peas, barley, lentils, carrots, turnip and tatties, all piping hot

But something was missing, it wasn't a bit like his ma's
Who knew in her wisdom, the basics of a good pot of soup lay in
    the stock
A big marrow bone or a mutton flank would have enhanced the taste
But she'd added plenty pepper and salt onyway
And made enough to last three days
But there was always the chip shop just two minutes' walk
Where you got a great fish supper, and why not?

By nineteen, she'd produced William, their son and heir
Once she'd got over the shock, she vowed she'd hae nae mair
Wi' her maternity grant she'd planned for herself a new coat
But Kirk Brothers were in dire need of a van
And were short o' a ten pound note

So it was ta-ta to that year's latest mode
A cardigan would have to do for going up the road
So five pounds were ear-marked to buy a second-hand pram
It was summer, And anyway, says Wullie, I'll keep you warm

These were the days, gie often skint
Five Players, a packet of wine gums and a night at the pictures
    was Myra's high-jinks
Sometimes she'd take wee William, who sat upon her knee
Sucking on his dummy, as good as could be
She soon made friends, she never complained
There were many who thought she'd never stay
    she'd want to go hame
But she showed them a', she never gave up the ghost
She surprised everyone, she never deserted her post

Then along came Margaret, their family complete
Myra's still residing in Cauther, queen of the street
She cooks and bakes, plays bools and bingo some days
She's never gives in, that's how Myra's made

By her side she's got Wullie, a staunch Scotsman is he
It goes to show the English and the Scots can get on fine
Though whiles at times no' agree

So here's tae them both, come what may
Take care of each other, what more can I say?

24 July 2004

Nell

If you believe in fairies, take a look at Nell
Hair like corn in summertime, eyes like wild bluebells
Surrounded by woodland, grassy knolls and dells
Cowslips, columbine, forget-me-nots, an ideal place where elves
    and fairies like to dwell

A place where you might meet the fairy king and queen
Like the Shakespearean play A Mid Summer Night's Dream
And fairies, if they feel inclined
Can be quite mischievous at times

Folklore tells how in the past
They appeared by magic in the grass
The bottom of the garden was their favourite place
They'd leave little boys and girls amazed

If you believe in fairies, and I'm sure you do
Maybe some day they will appear and sprinkle magic stardust
    over you
And if you're wondering what gift they bestowed on Nell
Was it her big blue eyes? Her pretty face? I think it was her smile

24 July 2004

Janet Meikle – 70th Birthday

We are gathered here to wish Janet a happy birthday, she is sev-
    enty years young
Her family have kindly invited us along to join in the fun

Thinking back over the years, tae the auld Foulshiels days
The world was young, so were we in the sixties

The hippies were in, make peace not war, flower power
We'd go guisin' each Halloween, happy times they were
We dooked for apples, in the auld tin bath, big folk, wee folk alike
Then Janet would get the byre brush, n' sweep the water
    an' monkey nuts
Oot the scullery door, oot o' sight

The entertainment wid begin, a joke, a poem, a song
While Davie kept the glasses topped up, it helped the sing-a-long
Andra gied us Kissin' In The Dark
Big Wullie and Rena, The Road And The Miles To Dundee
Michael, The Farmer's Boy, Mr Aitken's favourite, you see

Marion wid transport us to Glencoe, or maybe Loch Maree
An' if she felt like giein us an encore
The Old Rugged Cross always made Andra dash for the door
An' Jean wi' Big Wullie's Ingrowin' Toenail, her party piece
An', of course, mysel' wi' some long-winded tale, when we got
    a bit wheesht

Ina dressed up as an auld man, Jimmy dressed tae thrill
In female gear, caused quite a stir, I can see them still
Ellen in her Celtic strip, much younger then, of course
Complete wi' ba' and football boots
We laughed till we were hoarse

Jean and Issy dressed as hippies, sang a duet, Ye Banks And Braes
Bairns running a' ower the place, wi' sausage rolls
    pineapple cakes
Edward sittin' by the fireside, aye, he was dressed up an' a'
He always drove us back hame again
Tae that wee hoose Ower the Wa'

Mr and Mrs Aitken, the salt o' the earth, them two
Sat and watched the night's proceedings, and enjoyed
   the how-d'you-do

The years moved on, things changed, as they're inclined to do
Janet moved tae Stepend chicken farm as under-manager
   tae pastures new

She got on well wi' her workers, always there tae listen and advise
She had an empathy wi' the young folk
She's just no' a bonnie face, she's also very wise

Once again the years flew by, Jeanette and David flew the nest
Janet now was on her own, lookin' forward tae retirement
And a much-needed rest

By then she had Walter, remember him?
They'd go for midnight strolls the gither, they were an item
   her and him
Round about the rows of huts, like a sentry they went
Her guard dog by her side, Walter, her four-legged friend

Then along came the grandweans, whom she simply adores
In her wee but an' ben, now retired
She sometimes looks after a' four

An' again she's got that much patience, so tolerant and kind
Sorts oot any squabbles, without ever a slap on the behind
Janet tae loose her temper, I've yet got to see
I don't think she's got one, like you and me

She'd dae anything for anyone, so she will
Drives folk back an' forth tae the day-centre
Goes visiting them if they're ill

Maybe that's why she keeps young at heart
Or is it a' in the genes? For the whole family are like that

Anyway, Janet, today have fun
Wi' a' yer pals, while they're still able to come

2004

Flat 11, Dickson Court, Dickson Street

That's my new address
When folk ask if I like it here, the answer is, oh, yes
I've a nice wee upstairs flat, a room with a view
Equipped with all the latest technology
Helps keep us safe and sound, and of course, happy too

I came in here a year ago, on the fifth of May
Along with my favourite bits 'n' pieces
Settled in almost right away

My flat's at the front of Dickson Court
Facing the north-west
In the evening, if she's around
The sun pays a visit before she goes to rest

The sun sets later at this time of year
These long summer nights
The clouds as they shift and drift along
The planes flying to and fro before disappearing out of sight

I love that time of evening, relaxing sitting there
Grateful I have time, as they say, to stop and think and stare

June 2006

Hot Flushes

It was there when we arrived at the table
A notice in very large print so we could see
Saying the management were aware
Very hot water was coming from somewhere it ought not to be

So, now, what could have happened?
To date there is no answer as yet
In the meantime why not take the opportunity
While the toilet doubles as a bidet

So aren't we awfully lucky in Dickson Court?
In hygiene once again it's first class
No need for toilet paper, no hassle wiping your a**!

No doubt yet another notice will be issued
Saying the water system is back under control
Signed L. Currie, another snagging problem
Hopefully resolved

February 2007

Reminiscing in Dickson Court

Our childhood days, long gone
But still old memories linger on
The village school, blackboard, chalk
The wooden pointer, leather strap

The playground during intervals
Skipping ropes, tig, footballs
Swapping marbles, chestnuts on string
Shouting, laughing, arguing

Moving to High School
Making friends, growing fast
Leaving when we reached fourteen
To join the working class

By now, strange goings-on – Britain was at war
Being young we queried, why, where, what for?
School gates, railings confiscated
Also granny's pots and pans
Signposts removed, gas masks issued
Blackout throughout the land

Ration books, air-raid shelters, search lights in the sky
Warning posters – Careless Talk Costs Lives!
The neighbours might be spies!
The country on red alert, home guards, ARP
Troop movement day and night
Nurses, soldiers, evacuees

That was long ago
Memories gradually faded
Thankfully we were never invaded
Now we've grown old, we often step back and look
To a chapter in life now confined to history books
A very different world now, we still keep going on
Thanks to Housing With Care in West Lothian

Halloween

Every year at this time when the moon is ready to turn
Witches are out and about causing mischief, they think it's fun
They arrive on a broomstick, at the back, a black cat
A long, black cloak and a tall pointed hat

Folk are advised to keep out their way
They turn your milk sour, put hens off the lay
If you happen to meet one, avoid eye contact
She might turn you into a pumpkin just out of spite

They meet with other witches in a secluded spot
In a cauldron they make some kind of hot-pot
They throw in rats, snails, toads, puppy dogs' tails too
They seem to enjoy it, I wouldn't eat it, would you?

They sit in a circle on a three-legged stool
Dook for apples and monkey nuts, drink a can of Red Bull
Play hide and seek, blind man's buff
At times, light their clay pipe and have a wee puff

Then as the cock is beginning to crow
They get on their broomsticks, ready to go
Like swallows, all of a sudden they all disappear
You won't see them again until the same time next year

Len Jackson's 80th Birthday

Len was born the year after nineteen-ten
The youngest of twenty-three weans, there was nae birth control
    then
Doon in Sheffield it was, he first saw daylight
Born officially English but he's a Scotsman the night
Aye, those were the days, Len
Those happy auld days when
Wi' a' your brothers and sisters
Aye, life was a' right

As a laddie, he played football, kicked the can in the street
Played hockey, an' once a lass made him greet
She broke his nose, much to Len's dismay
He minds o' it yet, seems just like yesterday
Aye, those were the days, Len
Those happy auld days when
You ran wi' yer pals
An' happily played

At nineteen he came up tae good auld Scotland
He'd had enough o' they English, he could them nae mair stand
He excelled at all sports – horse riding, swimming, the lot
Ballroom dancing an' boxing, he was some bloke
Aye, those were the days, Len
Those happy auld days when
You were younger an' fit then
Happy was your lot

He fell in love an' got mairrit tae a bonnie wee lass
She put a stop tae his boxing she wanted his good looks tae last
Along came the family tae make his life complete

Twa strapping daughters – they live doon the street
Aye, those were the days, Len
Those happy auld days when
Wi' his family aroon' him
For him, life was sweet

He met his auld pal Bob Sorbie en route tae Algiers
They went through the war an' hae been freens for years
At fifty, his health took a turn for the worse
He survived a brain tumour
It came off the worst
Aye, remember those days, Len
It seems a long time when
You'd tae gie up your wee business
Your health it came first

Well, noo he's reached eighty an' heid o' the clan
Playing the role of Godfather as best as he can
His hair is noo grey and he's put on a bit weight
He still gets aroon but still misses his mate
Aye, life is still sweet, Len
You wouldna' change it agin when
You look back ower the years
Them you just canna bate

So we're a' here tonight tae wish him the best
Relations an' freens, grandweans and the rest
Many happy returns o' whit's left of the day
I hope you sleep soundly when we a' go away
And dreams o' the auld days, Len
Those happy auld days when
Life smiled on you kindly
An' left some grand memories

Isabella's Wardrobe

Sound the trumpet, blow the horn
In Crow Road, there's a new boutique born
Ali's in business, as from today
She's so happy, and she's done it her way

Since leaving Uni, she's used all her skills
Never been idle, paid all her bills
Jamie and Rory, are noo at the age
Eager to go on to the next phase

Now's the time to leave the past toil, trouble and strife
Begin a new chapter in her book of life
After being stuck in an office, managing the company's £SD
Making excuses to clients whose bills were overdue

I can picture her father, hands clenched, thumbs up
His way of saying, he's behind you, watching
Wishing you good luck
She'll meet lots of new people, perhaps maybe find somebody
    special, there's always a chance
One thing, they say, leads to another
I wonder maybe romance?

As yet she's no' met the man of her dreams
She's o'er busy building her empire, it seems
But never say never, there's always hope
That someday she'll meet a really nice bloke

So now's the time for her dreams and hopes
To come tumbling out, as she opens the door
Of Isabella's Wardrobe

August 2009

Andrew Ewing – 90th Birthday

Happy birthday, Andrew, you've seen quite a few
Did your bit for your country, in the Second World War too
A sailor, ever so smart, you at your best
A sweetheart in every port too, I bet

Until you met the girl of your dreams
Rather like Burns, you both married a bonnie Jean
Then came the chance, a new chapter to start
It's anchor up, and away for Australia you depart

Excitement, adventure, call it destiny or fate
Always optimistic, the future looked bloody great
Then eventually you arrived in the Promised Land
Got used to the climate, looking forward to do all you planned

Like waltzing Matilda, you keep moving on
Travelling light, a modern-day vagabond
Your worldly possessions crammed in your old van
You travelled the length and breadth of that vast land

Jack-of-all-trades, master of none
Willing and able, you old son-of-a-gun
They say a rolling stone gathers no moss
What you were gathering, something precious it was
A head filled with memories, if put down in script
Would make interesting reading
Why don't you try it?

Forty years in Australia, before returning to Scotland again
At least ten years left of your allotted lifespan
Here's wishing you health and happiness, my friend
Have a nice day on Tuesday from beginning to end

26 January 2010

Margaret Strachan

I hear you're sixty Margaret, you've no' long to go
I don't mean you're on your last legs, oh, dearie me, no!
I mean you'll soon be retired, footloose, fancy free
Able tae go tae a' they faraway places you aye longed to see

You could go tae China and see the Great Wall
See the Himalayas, Tibet or Nepal
Mount Everest is there but don't be tempted to go even part
    of the way
You could very well find yourself in Jeopardy
I'm not sure where that is, I think that's down Mexico way

Mind the last big hill ye went up, you couldna' get back doon again
Eddie was in a quandary, thought he'd gae ye a piggy-back then
    decided he wis too auld for that game
An' as you hadne been born wi' the wings o' a dove
The only other thing he could dae was brace hisel'
    and gie you a shove
You'd probably land in a clump o' nettles or a big jaggy bush
He'd be sure tae get lalday when you got back to the hoose

Why no' go for a quiet holiday, up tae Tiree?
It's a completely flat island, covered in wild flowers, butterflies
 an' bumbees
Plenty fawn and flora, the folk couthie an' kind
Aye, go there, while you're still in your prime

There's aye Japan, you could go tae Tokyo
Eddie in his kilt, wid cause a bigger sensation than Subo
They'd a' want his photo and his autograph
They'll be roon him like a swarm o' wasps

The Seychelles they say are nice
But pirates lurk there, you'd be kidnapped and held for ransom
 you'd better think twice
Even if we'd tae hae a whip roon it widna be enough
You'd need to try and outwit them, call their bluff

Tell them yer gaen up the galaxy, and you're waiting on a bus
That's where you came frae, in a wee place called Sagittarius
They'll take a look and say, They pair are off their chump
No' the full shilling, daft, naebody in their right minds would gie
 even a button to get them back
It's us that's in danger, an' as they've nothing tae plunder
Wait till their backs are turned, then we'll dae a runner!

I ken ain thing you'll no' dae, and that's nothing! You'll no' stop!
But if you've still got that new caravan you bought
There's yer answer staring you straight in the face
Go where and when you want tae, many happy returns, good health
 and good luck always

Benjamin

I'm a black and white collie, I answer to Ben
My official title is Kippriggs Benjamin
My mither was born on the Drumlong estate
Her title, the Duchess Kim
Her pups were mair or less spoken for before they were born
Sure enough, in time, one by one they had gone

They must ha' noticed by the time I was three
I hadn't whit it takes to become a great sheepdog, no' me
I had nae interest in sheep
Spent the day chasing hens and ma ain tail till I got tired
Then I'd lie doon for a sleep

They wondered maybe if I'd be any guid as a stud
I was taen on a visit, but whatever they'd hoped for, it didnae work

So back hame I went, jumping an' skipping a' the way
I heard them talking, sayin', You ken whit I think?
The bloody dug's gay
I'll say this, it's got a great pedigree
But it's nae dam guid, take it frae me

So I was sold tae an elderly couple for a hundred pounds, as a pet
For a guid sheep dug wid cost you aboot an arm an' a leg
They were an awfy nice couple, had a bit garden
An' a nice bungalow
Everything tae ma liking, everything so-so

Then ane day, there wis a right commotion, oh, dearie me
In comes the doctor, things were bad, I could see

BENJAMIN

I got shoved oot in the garden, oot o' the way
The puir soul didnae ken whit tae dae

Social Services came in to see whit the mistress would need
Grab-rails, etcetera, a ramp for a wheelchair
They were a great help indeed
There I wis, putting on weight, bored and depressed
I kent fine I was a pest
The maister had a' things tae dae, he was up to high doh
I couldn't tell hoo many times I wis telt, You'll have to go

He was thinking of phoning the Dogs Trust, see if they could find
    me a place
When in comes a joiner, tae see whit he had tae dae
When he learnt whit wis to happen tae me
He said he'd had a collie that had died recently
If my maister agreed, he'd love tae give me a hame
He would be welcome tae come, see where I'd be stayin'

Wid you believe it? An even bigger bungalow again
A big garden an' a'
A rabbit, four hens an' a fish pond, in it goldfish an' even minnows
Right oot the back there wis a track
Leading doon tae the Almond, ten minutes' walk

I wis fair gobsmacked, this wis ma lucky day
I let oot three big woof-woofs, that's dog language
    for hip-hip-hooray!
Ma auld maister came tae see hoo I had settled in
Said hoo much I was missed, wasn't that nice o' him?

So all's well that ends well, they say
Everything in the garden is rosy, I'm happy and gay

2011

List of Poems